Christmas
Please!

Christmas Please!

One Hundred Poems for the Festive Season

Edited by
Douglas Brooks-Davies

Illustrated by
Dan Williams

ORION

AN ORION PAPERBACK

First published in Great Britain in 2000 by Phoenix.
This edition published in 2003 by Orion
an imprint of Orion Books Ltd,
Orion House, 5 Upper St Martin's Lane, London WC2H 9EA

Introduction and selection © Phoenix Paperbacks, 2000
Illustrations copyright © Dan Williams, 2003

A CIP catalogue record for this book
is available from the British Library.

ISBN 0 75381 718 7

Printed and bound in Italy.

~ *Contents*

∼ *Introduction*

Memories of Christmas are precious things. A two-year-old will already remember the previous year's glittering tree; her (or his) grandmother will scarcely be able to distinguish that same tree from recollections of all previous family Christmas trees, evoking as they do the faces, laughter, and expectations of loved ones now grown old, or long dead. And if the radio happens to be on, maybe a carol or Christmas reading will prompt the aged mind to further thoughts of songs sung years since, or nativity plays once watched or acted in. Yet, although – or perhaps because – Christmas is compounded of so many personal memories, it also has a pre-dominant place in the collective folk memory, that mysterious space where Father Christmas and his reindeer rub shoulders with the infant Jesus, Mary and Joseph, shepherds are visited by angels, Herod slays boy babies, plum puddings and mince pies are devoured, yule logs are kindled, and a bright star shines in the black winter sky to be followed, year after year, by three mysterious Middle Eastern figures on their camels, bearing gifts of gold, frankincense, and myrrh through an improbably snowy landscape.

This is, of course, the raw material of the Christmas poem, and the hundred poems in this anthology touch on all aspects of Christmas, from the intimately personal to the more formally liturgical. Covering, as they do, a period of some six hundred years, from the fifteenth to the end of the twentieth century (the most recent poems are Gordon Snell's specially commissioned piece, and 'Advent Candle', written in December 1999 by eight-year-old Alexander Coulson), they offer a history of attitudes to Christmas and its various seasons: the penitential, preparatory season of Advent, which begins four Sundays before Christmas; Christmas itself; Epiphany (the manifestation of Christ to the three kings, commemorated on 6 January), and Candlemas, which commemorates, forty days after Christmas, on 2 February, the Purification of the Virgin Mary. This feast marked the end of Christmas in the medieval church, and was still popularly remembered as such in the seventeenth century (see the anonymous 'Carol, for Candlemas Day' included in this volume).

Broadly, what we observe from reading the poems presented here is a not surprising move, over the centuries, towards secularism and sentimentalism, and a blurring of distinct seasonal feasts into a general sense of Christmas as a short burst of eating, exchanging of gifts, celebrations of Virgin and Child, and an omnipresent Santa Claus – an American import who is apparently mentioned by name in Britain only as recently as the early nineteenth century. Clement Clark Moore's well-known 'A Visit from Saint Nicholas', with its list of Santa's reindeer, made its first appearance in print in New York on 23 December 1823.

Thus, the earliest poems (technically carols, with their celebratory narrative, uniform stanzas, and refrains) concentrate on the doctrine of the fall of man and Christ's redemptive birth, as in 'Out of the Blossom Sprang a Thorn' (which draws on the symbol of Mary as the mystic rose, and the tradition, rooted in Genesis 3, that thorns grew as the result of man's fall into sin). The blossom bears a thorn in this poem to show how sinless Christ takes man's sin to Himself: man is no longer lost, 'forlorn', because Christ will sacrifice Himself on the cross, His brow pierced by the crown of thorns which is at once the emblem of mankind's sinful nature and, through the shedding of redemptive blood, Christ's and man's triumph over death. The idea that Christ's death is present, symbolically, at the very moment of His birth is a Franciscan one; and, indeed, the crib itself, as we now know it, was introduced by St Francis in 1223, three years before his death. Almost as soon as it was placed in his hermitage in Grecchio it became a focus of adoration. Those who visited it knelt and sang lullabies before it, and the Franciscans who came to England in the thirteenth century to spread their message did so, by and large, through song. This is the origin of the nativity carol, and of the Christmas lullaby song.

Many early Christmas carols were written in two languages, English and Latin (the ensuing hybrid is usually known as macaronic verse). This is because the carol writers were drawing on the Latin Christmas liturgies of the Church, and interweaving the vernacular and priestly tongues in a way that was perfectly natural – even inevitable – if you spoke both with native ease. Some of these carols were written to be performed at ecclesiastical, collegiate, or aristocratic banquets; others may have been written for adorations at the crib, or to be incorporated into the processions which preceded the masses of the Christmas period. Not surprisingly, therefore, many of the Latin phrases in these poems were commonplaces derived from the Latin hymns which belonged to the liturgy, or from the Bible. As an aid to readers who may not be familiar with these poems, I offer, at the end of the volume, translations of Latin phrases that appear in poems printed in this anthology.

Macaronic verse disappears after the mid-sixteenth century as Protestantism, affirming the primacy of understanding over tradition, insists on the use of English in churches; and, as Christmas poems so often concentrated on the image of Virgin and Child, they tended to suffer as a genre from Protestantism's iconoclastic zeal, disappearing with the whitewashing of icons and smashing of images. The result is that the best sixteenth-century English Christmas poems are by Catholics (Robert Southwell; Henry Constable; and presumably the anonymous author of 'My Sweet Little Baby', published in the Catholic William Byrd's *Psalms, Sonets and Songs* of 1588), and belong to the Counter Reformation's attempt to repel Protestantism by all the propagandist means within its power. Similarly, the best seventeenth-century English Christmas poems are often either written by those who were Catholics for part of their lives (Ben Jonson, John Donne) or the product of the Anglo-Catholicism of Charles I and his Archbishop, Laud, and nostalgia for its disappearance as Puritanism established itself in the 1640s and 50s after the royalists lost the Civil War. The prime examples here are Richard Crashaw (who converted to Catholicism in the mid-1640s) and the poet cleric

Robert Herrick, who lost his Devon living under the Puritans, and writes almost obsessively of customs lost but still dear to memory. We might also add the anonymous poet who lamented that 'Old Christmas is kicked out of town' in the ballad 'Listen to me, and you shall hear', published in 1646.

Christmas poems weren't all written from the margins out of a sense of defeat or denial, however, as those included here by George Herbert, John Milton and Henry Vaughan amply demonstrate. But the Puritan downgrading of Christmas had its effect, spawning the Christmas poems of the later seventeenth century, which are mere secular celebrations of food and drink (see poems 89 and 92, which are from *Poor Robin's Almanac*).

The *Poor Robin* type of poem survived well into the next century, yet the arrival of congregational hymns in churches with the end of the seventeenth century prepared the way for the devotional offerings of, among others, Charles Wesley, John Byrom, and even the early Thomas Chatterton, within the following sixty years or so. The general paucity of Christmas poems from the eighteenth century, though, testifies to the fact that British (as opposed particularly to Lutheran) Protestants remained rather uninterested in Christmas.

In fact, Christmas really made its reappearance with the medieval yearnings of late eighteenth- and early nineteenth-century romanticism: for example, in that nostalgic passage from Walter Scott's *Marmion*, with its cry for a long-lost 'merry England' (or, in this case, Scotland) that is at least as deep and intense as any similar cry from the seventeenth century. This is Scott's anticipation of the festive Dickensian Christmas, itself a concoction of fantasy, remembered history, and wish-fulfilment, the time when that never actually was. Because (to return to my beginning) Christmas carries such a freight of memory to all except the very young that it becomes a metaphor for loss and remembered happiness. Hence, at around the same time as Scott, William Wordsworth swings from present to past, and a shared 'simple childhood', as he writes a Christmas verse epistle to his absent brother; and, later, Tennyson remembers with anguish, as the Christmas bells ring out once more, the death of his beloved Arthur Hallam; Mathilde Blind feels her solitude; and Thomas Hardy reflects predictably (but nonetheless movingly) on what, in 'The Dead Quire', he calls 'The Mead of Memories'.

And, of course, less gloomily, we have Clement Clark Moore's 'A Visit from St Nicholas', William Barnes's winking assurance that romping with the girls, playing games and drinking ale will help 'keep wold Chris'mas up', and the 'Glad Christmas' of John Clare's *The Shepherd's Calendar* (1827), with its glorious perception of snow as celestial goose feathers:

> And some, to view the winter weathers,
>   Climb up the window-seat with glee,
> Likening the snow to falling feathers
>   In Fancy's infant ecstasy;
> Laughing, with superstitious love,
>   O'er visions wild that youth supplies,
> Of people pulling geese above
>   And keeping Christmas in the skies.

Equally, the nineteenth century, under the influence especially of the High Church Oxford Movement (equivalent in religious and poetic terms to the Laudian Anglo-Catholic position of England under Charles I) brought us some fine religious Christmas poems. John Keble (1792–1866), Oxford professor of poetry and chief spokesman for the Movement, popularly defined and exemplified the new spirituality in his poetic calendar *The Christian Year*, published anonymously in the same year as John Clare's more secular vignettes of the months; and his inheritance can be detected in, for instance, the High Church Christina Rossetti's 'Advent', a poem almost perfect in its linguistic simplicity and in its exploration of the advent themes of quiet waiting and watching for the arrival of Christ the bridegroom (hence her concluding quotation, after an earlier allusion to the parable of the virgins and their lamps in Matthew 25, from that great biblical marriage poem, the Song of Solomon, 2:10: 'Arise, My love, My fair one, come away'); while the Oxonian John Addington Symonds's little known 'A Christmas Lullaby' is an utterly lovely crib devotion.

But there is no need to go on enumerating. The poems in this anthology have been chosen because they are all, in their own way, special: all touch on a mixture of emotions as they ponder the implications of John Betjeman's question in his poem 'Christmas':

And is it true? And is it true,
    This most tremendous tale of all,
Seen in a stained-glass window's hue,
    A Baby in an ox's stall?
The Maker of the stars and sea
Become a Child on earth for me?

DOUGLAS BROOKS-DAVIES

Christmas
Please!

'I Sing of a Maiden'
(fifteenth century)

I sing of a maiden that is makeless,
King of all kings to her Son she ches.

He came also stilly there His mother was:
As dew in Aprillè, that falleth on the grass.

He came also stilly to His mother's bower,
As dew in Aprillè that falleth on the flower.

He came also stilly where His mother lay,
As dew in Aprillè, that falleth on the spray.

Mother and maiden was never none but she –
Well may such a lady God's mother be!

'Lullay, Mine Liking'

(fifteenth century)

    'Lullay, mine liking, my dear son, mine sweeting,
    Lullay, mine dear heart, mine own dear darling.'

I saw a fair maiden sitten and sing:
She lullayed a little child, a sweet lording.

That each Lord is that that made allè thing;
Of all lords he is Lord, of all kingès King.

There was mickle melody at that Child's birth,
Although they were in heaven's bliss, they made mickle mirth.

Angels bright they sang that night, and saiden to that Child:
'Blessed be Thou, and blessed be she that is both meek and
   mild.'

Pray we now to that Child, and to His mother dear,
Grant them His blessing that now maken cheer.

'Out of the Blossom Sprang a Thorn'

(fifteenth century)

Out of the blossom sprang a thorn
When God himself would be born –
He let us never be forlorn
   That born was of Mary.

There sprang a well at her foot
That all this world it turned to good,
When Jesu Christ took flesh and blood
   Of His mother Mary.

Out of the well sprang a stream
From patriarch to Jerusalem,
Till Christ Himself again it nem
   Of His mother Mary.

In winter when the frost Him froze
A poor bedding our Lord Him chose
Between an ox and an ass:
God's Son born He was
   Of His mother Mary.

It was upon the Twelfth Day
There came three kings in rich array,
To seek Christ where He lay,
   And His mother Mary.

Three kings out of diverse land
Swithè camen with hertè strong
The Child to seeken and underfong
   That born was of Mary.

The star led them a right way
To the Child where He lay –
He helps us both night and day
   That born was of Mary.

Balthazar was the firstè king:
He brought gold to his offering
For to present that richè King
   And His mother Mary.

Melchior was the second king:
He brought incense to his offering
For to present that richè King
   And His mother Mary.

Jasper was the third king:
He brought myrrh to his offering
For to present that richè King
   And His mother Mary.

There they offered their presents
With gold and myrrh and frankincense,
As clerkès readen in their sequence
   In Epiphany.

Kneel we down Him beforn,
And pray we to Him that now is born
He let us never be forlorn
   That born was of Mary.

Chris'mas Invitation

Come down tomorrow night; an' mind,
Don't leave thy fiddle-bag behind;
We'll sheäke a lag, an' drink a cup
O' eäle, to keep wold Chris'mas up.

An' let thy sister teäke thy eärm,
The walk won't do her any harm;
There's noo dirt now to spweil her frock,
The ground's a-vroze so hard's a rock.

You won't meet any stranger's feäce,
But only naïghbours o' the pleäce,
An' Stowe, an' Combe; and two or dree
Vrom uncle's up at Rookery.

An' thou wu'lt vind a rwosy feäce,
An' peäir ov eyes so black as sloos,
The prettiest woones in all the pleäce, –
I'm sure I needen tell thee whose.

We got a back-bran', dree girt logs
So much as dree ov us can car;
We'll put em up athirt the dogs,
An' meäke a vier to the bar.

An' ev'ry woone shall tell his teäle,
An' ev'ry woone shall zing his zong,
An' ev'ry woone wull drink his eäle
To love an' frien'ship all night long.

We'll snap the tongs, we'll have a ball,
We'll sheäke the house, we'll lift the ruf,
We'll romp an' meäke the maïdens squall,
A-catchen o'm at blind-man's buff.

Zoo come tomorrow night; an' mind,
Don't leäve thy fiddle-bag behind;
We'll sheäke a lag, an' drink a cup
O' eäle, to keep wold Chris'mas up.

Christmas

The bells of waiting Advent ring,
  The Tortoise stove is lit again
And lamp-oil light across the night
  Has caught the streaks of winter rain
In many a stained-glass window sheen
From Crimson Lake to Hooker's Green.

The holly in the windy hedge
  And round the Manor House the yew
Will soon be stripped to deck the ledge,
  The altar, font and arch and pew,
So that the villagers can say
'The church looks nice' on Christmas Day.

Provincial public houses blaze
  And Corporation tramcars clang,
On lighted tenements I gaze
  Where paper decorations hang,
And bunting in the red Town Hall
Says 'Merry Christmas to you all.'

And London shops on Christmas Eve
    Are strung with silver bells and flowers
As hurrying clerks the City leave
    To pigeon-haunted classic towers,
And marbled clouds go scudding by
The many-steepled London sky.

And girls in slacks remember Dad,
    And oafish louts remember Mum,
And sleepless children's hearts are glad,
    And Christmas-morning bells say 'Come!'
Even to shining ones who dwell
Safe in the Dorchester Hotel.

And is it true? And is it true,
    This most tremendous tale of all,
Seen in a stained-glass window's hue,
    A Baby in an ox's stall?
The Maker of the stars and sea
Become a Child on earth for me?

And is it true? For if it is,
    No loving fingers tying strings
Around those tissued fripperies,
    The sweet and silly Christmas things,
Bath salts and inexpensive scent
And hideous tie so kindly meant,

No love that in a family dwells,
    No carolling in frosty air,
Nor all the steeple-shaking bells
    Can with this simple truth compare –
That God was Man in Palestine
And lives today in Bread and Wine.

A Cradle Song

Sweet dreams form a shade
O'er my lovely infant's head:
Sweet dreams of pleasant streams
By happy, silent moony beams.

Sweet sleep with soft down
Weave thy brows an infant crown;
Sweet sleep, angel mild,
Hover o'er my happy child.

Sweet smiles in the night,
Hover over my delight;
Sweet smiles, mother's smiles,
All the livelong night beguiles.

Sweet moans, dovelike sighs,
Chase not slumber from thy eyes;
Sweet moans, sweeter smiles,
All the dovelike moans beguiles.

Sleep, sleep, happy child;
All creation slept and smiled;
Sleep, sleep, happy sleep,
While o'er thee thy mother weep.

Sweet babe, in thy face
Holy image I can trace:
Sweet babe, once like thee
Thy Maker lay and wept for me.

Wept for me, for thee, for all
When He was an infant small:
Thou His image ever see,
Heavenly face that smiles on thee.

Smiles on me, on thee, on all,
Who became an infant small:
Infant smiles are His own smiles,
Heaven and earth to peace beguiles.

Christmas Eve

Alone – with one fair star for company,
The loveliest star among the hosts of night,
While the grey tide ebbs with the ebbing light –
I pace along the darkening wintry sea.
Now round the yule-log and the glittering tree
Twinkling with festive tapers, eyes as bright
Sparkle with Christmas joys and young delight,
As each one gathers to his family.

But I – a waif on earth where'er I roam –
Uprooted with life's bleeding hopes and fears
From that one heart that was my heart's sole home
Feel the old pang pierce through the severing years,
And as I think upon the years to come
That fair star trembles through my falling tears.

The Shepherd's Song:
A Carol or Hymn for Christmas

Sweet music, sweeter far
Than any song is sweet –
Sweet music heavenly rare
Mine ears (O peers) doth greet.
You gentle flocks, whose fleeces pearled with dew
Resemble heaven, whom golden drops make bright,
Listen, O listen: now O not to you
Our pipes make sport to shorten weary night,
But voices most divine
Make blissful harmony:
Voices that seem to shine,
For what else clears the sky?
Tunes can we hear, but not the singers see:
The tunes divine, and so the singers be.

Lo how the firmament
Within an azure fold
The flock of stars hath pent
That we might them behold.
Yet from their beams proceedeth not this light,
Nor can their crystal such reflection give:
What, then, doth make the element so bright? –
The heavens are come down upon earth to live.
But hearken to the song:
'Glory to glory's King
And peace all men among'
These choristers do sing.
Angels they are, as also (shepherds) He
Whom in our fear we do admire to see.

'Let not amazement blind
Your souls' (said he) 'annoy:
To you and all mankind
My message bringeth joy.
For, lo, the world's great Shepherd now is born
A blessed Babe, an Infant full of power.'
After long night, uprisen is the morn
Renowning Bethlehem in the Saviour.
Sprung is the perfect day,
By prophets seen afar:
Sprung is the mirthful May
Which winter cannot mar;
In David's city doth this Sun appear
Clouded in flesh, yet, shepherds, sit we here.

Noel: Christmas Eve, 1913
Pax hominibus bonae voluntatis

A frosty Christmas Eve
 when the stars were shining
Fared I forth alone
 where westward falls the hill,
And from many a village
 in the water'd valley
Distant music reached me
 peals of bells aringing:
The constellated sounds
 ran sprinkling on earth's floor
As the dark vault above
 with stars was spangled o'er.

Then sped my thought to keep
 that first Christmas of all
When the shepherds watching
 by their folds ere the dawn
Heard music in the fields
 and marvelling could not tell
Whether it were angels
 or the bright stars singing.

Now blessed be the tow'rs
 that crown England so fair
That stand up strong in prayer
 unto God for our souls:
Blessed be their founders
 (said I) an' our country folk
Who are ringing for Christ
 in the belfries to-night
With arms lifted to clutch
 the rattling ropes that race
Into the dark above
 and the mad romping din.

But to me heard afar
   it was starry music
Angels' song, comforting
   as the comfort of Christ
When he spake tenderly
   to his sorrowful flock:
The old words came to me
   by the riches of time
Mellow'd and transfigured
   as I stood on the hill
Heark'ning in the aspect
   of th'eternal silence.

Christmas Eve, 1917

Many happy returns, sweet Babe, of the day!
Didst not thou sow good seed in the world, thy field?
Cam'st thou to save the poor? Thy poor yet pine.
Thousands to-day suffer death-pangs like thine;
Our jewels of life are spilt on the ground as dross;
Ten thousand mothers stand beneath the cross.
Peace to men of good will was the angels' song:
Now there is fiercer war, worse filth and wrong.
If thou didst sow good seed, is this the yield?
Shall not thy folk be quell'd in dead dismay?

Nay, with a larger hope we are fed and heal'd
Than e'er was reveal'd to the saints who died so strong;
For while men slept the seed had quicken'd unseen.
England is as a field whereon the corn is green.

Of trial and dark tribulation this vision is born –
Britain as a green field with the springing corn.
While we slumber'd the seed was growing unseen.
Happy returns of the day, dear Babe, we say.

ENGLAND has buried her sins with her fathers' bones.
Thou shalt be throned on the ruin of kingly thrones.
The wish of thine heart is rooted in carnal mind;
For good seed didst thou sow in the world thy field:
It shall ripen in gold and harvest an hundredfold.
Peace shall come as a flood upon all mankind;
Love shall comfort and succour the poor that are pined.

Wherever our gentle children are wander'd and sped,
Simple apostles thine of the world to come,
They carried the living seed of the living Bread,
The angel-song and gospel of Christendom,
That while the nation slept was springing unseen.

So tho' we be sorely stricken we feel no dread:
Our thousand sons suffer death-pangs like thine:
It shall ripen in gold and harvest an hundredfold:
Peace and Love shall hallow our care and teen,
Shall bind in fellowship all the folk of the earth
To kneel at thy cradle, Babe, and bless thy birth.

Ring we the bells up and down in country and town,
And keep the old feast unholpen of preacher or priest,
Wishing thee happy returns, and thy Mother May,
Ever happier and happier returns, dear CHRIST, of thy day!

Music on Christmas Morning

Music I love – but never strain
Could kindle raptures so divine,
So grief assuage, so conquer pain,
And rouse this pensive heart of mine –
As that we hear on Christmas morn,
Upon the wintry breezes borne.

Though Darkness still her empire keep,
And hours must pass ere morning break,
From troubled dreams, or slumbers deep,
That music kindly bids us wake:
It calls us, with an angel's voice,
To wake, and worship, and rejoice;

To greet with joy the glorious morn,
Which angels welcomed long ago,
When our redeeming Lord was born,
To bring the light of heaven below,
The powers of darkness to dispel,
And rescue earth from death and hell.

While listening to that sacred strain,
My raptured spirit soars on high;
I seem to hear those songs again
Resounding through the open sky,
That kindle such divine delight
In those who watched their flocks by night.

With them I celebrate His birth –
Glory to God in highest heaven,
Good-will to men, and peace on earth,
To us a Saviour-king is given;
Our God is come to claim His own,
And Satan's power is overthrown!

A sinless God for sinful men
Descends to suffer and to bleed;
Hell must renounce its empire then;
The price is paid, the world is freed,
And Satan's self must now confess
That Christ has earned a right to bless:

Now holy Peace may smile from heaven,
And heavenly Truth from earth shall spring:
The captive's galling bonds are riven,
For our Redeemer is our King;
And He that gives His blood for men
Will lead us home to God again.

Carol

Three kings from out the Orient
For Judah's land were fairly bent,
 To find the Lord of grace;
And as they journeyed pleasantlie,
A star kept shining in the sky,
 To guide them to the place.
'O Star,' they cried, 'by all confest
Withouten dreed, the loveliest!'

The first was Melchior to see
The emperour hight of Arabye,
 An aged man, I trow:
He sat upon a rouncy bold,
Had taken of the red red gold,
 The babe for to endow.
'O Star,' he cried, 'by all confest,
Withouten dreed, the loveliest!'

The next was Caspar, young and gay,
That held the realm of far Cathay –
      Our Jesus drew him thence –
Yclad in silk from head to heel,
He rode upon a high cameel,
      And bare the frankincense.
'O Star,' he cried, 'by all confest,
Withouten dreed, the loveliest!'

The last was dusky Balthasar,
That rode upon a dromedar –
      His coat was of the fur.
Dark-browed he came from Samarkand,
The Christ to seek, and in his hand
      Upheld the bleeding myrrh.
'O Star,' he cried, 'by all confest
Withouten dreed, the loveliest!'

The Virgin Mary to the Child Jesus

But see, the virgin blest
Hath laid her Babe to rest.
  – Milton's *Hymn on the Nativity*

    Sleep, sleep, mine Holy One,
My flesh, my Lord! What name? I do not know
A name that seemeth not too high or low,
    Too far from me or heaven:
My Jesus, *that* is best; that word being given
By the majestic angel, whose command
Was softly as a man's beseeching said,
When I and all the earth appeared to stand
    In the great overflow
Of light celestial from his wings and head.
    Sleep, sleep, my saving One!

And art Thou come for saving, baby-browed
And speechless Being – art Thou come for saving?
The palm that grows beside our door is bowed
By treadings of the low wind from the south,
A restless shadow through the chamber waving:
Upon its bough a bird sings in the sun,
But Thou, with that close slumber on Thy mouth,
Dost seem of wind and sun already weary.
Art come for saving, O my weary One?

Perchance this sleep that shutteth out the dreary
Earth-sounds and motions, opens on Thy soul
    High dreams on fire with God;
High songs that make the pathways where they roll
More bright than stars do theirs; and visions new
Of Thine eternal nature's old abode.

Suffer this mother's kiss,
Best thing that earthly is,
To glide the music and the glory through,
Nor narrow in Thy dream the broad upliftings
Of any seraph wing.
Thus noiseless, thus. Sleep, sleep, my dreaming One!

The slumber of His lips me seems to run
Through *my* lips to mine heart, to all its shiftings
Of sensual life, bringing contrariousness
In a great calm. I feel I could lie down
As Moses did, and die – and then live most.
I am 'ware of you, heavenly presences,
That stand with your peculiar light unlost,
Each forehead with a high thought for a crown,
Unsunned i' the sunshine! I am 'ware. Ye throw
No shade against the wall! How motionless
Ye round me with your living statuary,
While through your whiteness, in and outwardly,
Continual thoughts of God appear to go,
Like light's soul in itself. I bear, I bear
To look upon the dropped lids of your eyes,
Though their external shining testifies
To that beatitude within which were
Enough to blast an eagle at his sun:
I fall not on my sad clay face before ye, –
I look on His. I know
My spirit, which dilateth with the woe
Of His mortality,
May well contain your glory.
Yea, drop your lids more low:
Ye are but fellow-worshippers with me!
Sleep, sleep, my worshipped One!

We sat among the stalls at Bethlehem;
The dumb kine, from their fodder turning them,
     Softened their horned faces
     To almost human gazes
     Toward the newly-born;
The simple shepherds from the star-lit brooks
     Brought visionary looks:
As yet in their astonied hearing rung
     The strange, sweet angel tongue;
The magi of the east, in sandals worn,
     Knelt reverent, sweeping round,
With long, pale beards, their gifts upon the ground,
     The incense, myrrh and gold
These baby hands were impotent to hold:
So let all earthlies and celestials wait
     Upon Thy royal state.
     Sleep, sleep, my kingly One!

I am not proud – meek angels, ye invest
New meekness to hear such utterance rest
On mortal lips, – 'I am not proud' – *not proud!*
Albeit in my flesh God sent His Son,
Albeit over Him my head is bowed
As others bow before Him, still mine heart
Bows lower than their knees. O centuries
That roll in vision your futurities
     My future grave athwart, –
Whose murmurs seem to reach me while I keep
     Watch o'er this sleep, –
Say of me as the heavenly said: 'Thou art
The blessedest of women!' – blessedest,
Not holiest, not noblest, no high name
Whose height misplaced may pierce me like a shame
When I sit meek in heaven!
                  For me, for me,
God knows that I am feeble like the rest!
I often wandered forth, more child than maiden,

Among the midnight hills of Galilee
     Whose summits looked heaven-laden,
Listening to silence as it seemed to be
God's voice, so soft yet strong, so fain to press
Upon my heart as heaven did on the height,
And waken up its shadows by a light,
And show its vileness by a holiness.
Then I knelt down most silent like the night,
     Too self-renounced for fears,
Raising my small face to the boundless blue
Whose stars did mix and tremble in my tears:
God heard *them* falling after, with His dew.

So, seeing my corruption, can I see
This Incorruptible now born of me,
This fair new Innocence no sun did chance
To shine on (for even Adam was no child),
Created from my nature all defiled,
This mystery, from out mine ignorance, –
Nor feel the blindness, stain, corruption, more
Than others do, or *I* did heretofore?
Can hands wherein such burden pure has been,
Not open with the cry, 'unclean, unclean,'
More oft than any else beneath the skies?
     Ah, King, ah, Christ, ah son!
The kine, the shepherds, the abased wise
     Must all less lowly wait
     Than I, upon thy state.
    Sleep, sleep, my kingly One!

Art Thou a King, then? Come, His universe,
Come, crown me Him a King!
Pluck rays from all such stars as never fling
   Their light where fell a curse,
And make a crowning for this kingly brow! –
What is my word? Each empyreal star
     Sits in a sphere afar

In shining ambuscade:
The child-brow, crowned by none,
Keeps its unchildlike shade.
Sleep, sleep, my crownless One!

Unchildlike shade! No other babe doth wear
An aspect very sorrowful, as Thou.
No small babe-smiles my watching heart has seen
To float like speech the speechless lips between,
No dovelike cooing in the golden air,
No quick, short joys of leaping babyhood.
     Alas, our earthly good,
In heaven thought evil, seems too good for Thee:
     Yet, sleep, my weary One!

And then the drear, sharp tongue of prophecy,
With the dread sense of things which shall be done,
Doth smite me inly like a sword: a sword?
That 'smites the Shepherd'. Then, I think aloud
The words 'despised', 'rejected': every word
Recoiling into darkness as I view
     The darling on my knee.
Bright angels, move not, lest ye stir the cloud
Betwixt my soul and His futurity!
I must not die, with mother's work to do,
     And could not live – and see.

     It is enough to bear
     This image still and fair,
     This holier in sleep
     Than a saint at prayer,
     This aspect of a child
     Who never sinned or smiled;
     This Presence in an infant's face;
     This sadness most like love,
     This love than love more deep,
     This weakness like omnipotence
     It is so strong to move.

Awful is this watching-place,
Awful what I see from hence –
A King, without regalia,
A God, without the thunder,
A Child, without the heart for play;
Ay, a Creator, rent asunder
From His first glory, and cast away
On His own world, for me alone
To hold in hands created, crying 'Son'.

That tear fell not on Thee,
Beloved, yet Thou stirrest in Thy slumber.
Thou, stirring not for glad sounds out of number,
Which through the vibratory palm-trees run
From summer wind and bird,
So quickly hast Thou heard
A tear fall silently?
Wakest Thou, O loving One?

Hymn for Christmas Day

Christians awake, salute the happy morn,
Whereon the Saviour of the world was born;
Rise, to adore the mystery of love,
Which hosts of angels chanted from above:
With them the joyful tidings first begun
Of God incarnate, and the Virgin's Son.
Then to the watchful shepherds it was told,
Who heard the angelic herald's voice: 'Behold!
I bring good tidings of a Saviour's birth,
To you, and all the nations upon earth!
This day hath God fulfilled His promised Word;
This day is born a Saviour, Christ, the Lord.
In David's city, shepherds, ye shall find
The long foretold redeemer of mankind;
Wrapped up in swaddling clothes, the babe divine
Lies in a manger: this shall be your sign.'
He spake, and straightway the celestial choir,
In hymns of joy unknown before, conspire:
The praises of redeeming love they sung,
And heaven's whole orb with hallelujahs rung.
God's highest glory was their anthem still;
Peace upon earth and mutual good will.
To Bethlehem straight the enlightened shepherds ran,
To see the wonder God had wrought for man;
And found, with Joseph and the blessed maid,
Her Son, the Saviour, in a manger laid.
Amazed, the wondrous story they proclaim –
The first apostles of His infant fame:
While Mary keeps, and ponders in her heart,
The heavenly vision which the swains impart,
They to their flocks, still praising God, return,
And their glad hearts within their bosoms burn.

Let us, like these good shepherds then, employ
Our grateful voices to proclaim the joy:
Like Mary, let us ponder in our mind
God's wondrous love in saving lost mankind;
Artless and watchful as these favoured swains,
While virgin meekness in the heart remains:
Trace we the babe, who has retrieved our loss,
From His poor manger to His bitter cross;
Treading His steps, assisted by His grace,
Till man's first heavenly state again takes place.
Then may we hope the angelic thrones among
To sing, redeemed, a glad triumphal song.
He that was born upon this joyful day
Around us all His glory shall display;
Saved by His love, incessant we shall sing
Of angels, and of angel-men, the King.

'Adam Lay Ybounden'

(fifteenth century)

Adam lay ybounden, bounden in a bond:
Four thousand winter thought he not too long.

And all was for an apple, an apple that he took,
As clerkès finden written in their book.

Ne had the apple taken been, the apple taken been,
Ne had never Our Lady a been heavenè queen.

Blessed be the time that apple taken was:
Therefore we mown singen *Deo gracias*.

A Hymn for Christmas Day

Almighty Framer of the skies,
O let our pure devotion rise
    Like incense in Thy sight!
Wrapped in impenetrable shade
The texture of our souls were made
    Till Thy command gave light.

The Sun of Glory gleamed the ray,
Refined the darkness into day,
    And bid the vapours fly:
Impelled by His eternal love
He left the palaces above
    To cheer our gloomy sky.

How shall we celebrate the day
When God appeared in mortal clay,
    The mark of worldly scorn;
When the archangels' heavenly lays
Attempted the Redeemer's praise,
    And hailed salvation's morn?

A humble form the Godhead wore;
The pains of poverty He bore,
    To gaudy pomp unknown:
Though in a human walk He trod,
Still was the man almighty God
    In glory all His own.

Despised, oppressed, the Godhead bears
The torments of this vale of tears;
   Nor bid His vengeance rise:
He saw the creatures He had made
Revile His power, His peace invade –
   He saw with Mercy's eyes.

How shall we celebrate His name
Who groaned beneath a life of shame,
   In all afflictions tried?
The soul is raptured to conceive
A truth which being must believe:
   The God eternal died.

My soul, exert thy powers: adore;
Upon Devotion's plumage soar
   To celebrate the day:
The God from whom creation sprung
Shall animate my grateful tongue –
   From Him I'll catch the lay!

A Child of the Snows

There is heard a hymn when the panes are dim,
    And never before or again,
When the nights are strong with a darkness long,
    And the dark is alive with rain.

Never we know but in sleet and in snow,
    The place where the great fires are,
That in the midst of the earth is a raging mirth
    And the heart of the earth is a star.

And at night we win to the ancient inn
    Where the child in the frost is furled,
We follow the feet where all souls meet
    At the inn at the end of the world.

The gods lie dead where the leaves lie red,
    For the flame of the sun is flown;
The gods lie cold where the leaves lie gold,
    And a Child comes forth alone.

December
from *The Shepherd's Calendar*

Glad Christmas comes, and every hearth
   Makes room to give him welcome now,
E'en Want will dry its tears in mirth,
   And crown him with a holly bough;
Though tramping 'neath a winter sky,
   O'er snowy paths and rimy stiles,
The housewife sets her spinning by
   To bid him welcome with her smiles.

Each house is swept the day before,
   And windows stuck with evergreens;
The snow is besomed from the door,
   And comfort crowns the cottage scenes.
Gilt holly, with its thorny pricks,
   And yew and box, with berries small,
These deck the unused candlesticks,
   And pictures hanging by the wall ...

The block upon the fire is put,
   To sanction custom's old desires,
And many a faggot's bands are cut
   For the old farmers' Christmas fires,
Where loud-tongued Gladness joins the throng,
   And Winter meets the warmth of May
Till, feeling soon the heat too strong,
   He rubs his shins and draws away.

While snows the window-panes bedim
    The fire curls up, a sunny charm,
Where, creaming o'er the pitcher's rim,
    The flowering ale is set to warm.
Mirth, full of joy as summer bees,
    Sits there, its pleasures to impart,
And children, 'tween their parents' knees,
    Sing scraps of carols o'er by heart.

And some, to view the winter weathers,
    Climb up the window-seat with glee,
Likening the snow to falling feathers
    In Fancy's infant ecstasy;
Laughing, with superstitious love,
    O'er visions wild that youth supplies,
Of people pulling geese above
    And keeping Christmas in the skies.

As though the homestead tree were dressed,
    In lieu of snow, with dancing leaves;
As though the sun-dried martin's nest,
    Instead of icicles, hung the eaves,
The children hail the happy day,
    As if the snow were April's grass;
And pleased, as 'neath the warmth of May,
    Sport o'er the water froze to glass.

Thou day of happy sound and mirth,
    That long with childish memory stays,
How blest around the cottage hearth
    I met thee in my younger days!
Harping, with rapture's dreaming joys,
    On presents which thy coming found,
The welcome sight of little toys,
    The Christmas gifts of comers round.

The wooden horse with arching head,
   Drawn upon wheels around the room;
The gilded coach of gingerbread,
   And many-coloured sugar plum;
Gilt covered books for pictures sought,
   Of stories childhood loves to tell,
With many an urgent promise bought
   To get tomorrow's lesson well.

And many a thing, a minute's sport,
   Left broken on the sanded floor,
When we would leave our play, and court
   Our parents' promises for more.
Though manhood bids such raptures die,
   And throws such toys aside as vain,
Yet memory loves to turn her eye,
   And count past pleasures o'er again.

Around the glowing hearth at night
   The harmless laugh and winter tale
Go round, while parting friends delight
   To toast each other o'er their ale;
The cotter oft with quiet zeal
   Will musing o'er his Bible lean;
While in the dark the lovers steal
   To kiss and toy behind the screen.

Old customs! Oh, how I love the sound,
   However simple they may be:
Whate'er with time hath sanction found
   Is welcome, and is dear to me.
Pride grows above simplicity,
   And spurns them from her haughty mind;
And soon the poet's song will be
   The only refuge they can find.

Repose in Egypt

O happy mother, while the man wayworn
Sleeps by his ass and dreams of daily bread,
Wakeful and heedful for thy Infant thou,
O happy mother, while thy husband sleeps,
Art privileged, O blessed one, to see
Celestial strangers sharing in thy task,
And visible angels waiting on thy Child.

Take, O young soul, O Infant heaven-desired,
Take and fear not the cates, although of earth,
Which to Thy hands celestial hands extend.
Take and fear not: such vulgar meats of life
Thy spirit lips no more must scorn to pass;
The seeming ill, contaminating joys,
Thy sense divine no more be loth to allow.
The pleasures as the pains of our strange life
Thou art engaged, self-compromised, to share.
Look up! Upon Thy mother's face there sits
No sad suspicion of a lurking ill,
No shamed confession of a needful sin.
Mistrust her not, albeit of earth she too.
Look up! The bright-eyed cherubs overhead
Show from mid air fresh flowers to crown the feast.
Look! Thy own father's servants these, and Thine,
Who at His bidding and at Thine are here.
In Thine own words was it not said long since,
Butter and honey shall he eat, and learn
The evil to refuse and choose the good?
Fear not, O Babe divine, fear not, accept.
O happy mother, privileged to see,
While the man sleeps, the sacred mystery.

'I Saw a Stable'

I saw a stable, low and very bare,
  A little Child in a manger.
The oxen knew Him, had Him in their care,
  To men He was a stranger.
The safety of the world was lying there,
  And the world's danger.

The Virgin's Cradle Hymn

Dormi, Jesu! Mater ridet
Quae tam dulcem somnum videt;
Dormi, Jesu, blandule!
Si non dormis, Mater plorat,
Inter fila cantans orat:
Blande, veni, somnule.

English

Sleep, sweet babe, my cares beguiling;
Mother sits beside Thee, smiling;
Sleep, my darling, tenderly!
If Thou sleep not, mother mourneth,
Singing as her wheel she turneth:
Come, soft slumber, balmily!

A Christmas Carol

The shepherds went their hasty way,
   And found the lowly cattle shed
Where the virgin mother lay:
   And now they check their eager tread,
For to the babe, that at her bosom clung,
A mother's song the virgin mother sung.

They told her how a glorious light,
   Streaming from a heavenly throng,
Around them shone, suspending night!
   While sweeter than a mother's song
Blest angels heralded the Saviour's birth:
'Glory to God on high, and peace on earth!'

She listened to the tale divine,
   And closer still the babe she pressed;
And while she cried 'The Babe is mine!',
   The milk rushed faster to her breast:
Joy rose within her like a summer morn:
Peace, peace on earth! The Prince of Peace is born!

Thou mother of the Prince of Peace,
   Poor, simple, and of low estate!
That strife should vanish, battle cease,
   O why should this thy soul elate?
Sweet music's loudest note, the poet's story –
Didst thou ne'er love to hear of fame and glory?

And is not War a youthful king,
   A stately hero clad in mail?
Beneath his footsteps laurels spring;
   Him earth's majestic monarchs hail
Their friend, their playmate! And his bold, bright eye
Compels the maiden's love-confessing sigh.

'Tell this in some more courtly scene
    To maids and youths in robes of state!
I am a woman poor and mean,
    And therefore is my soul elate.
War is a ruffian, all with guilt defiled,
That from the aged father tears his child.

'A murderous fiend, by fiends adored,
    He kills the sire and starves the son;
The husband kills, and from her board
    Steals all his widow's toil had won;
Plunders God's world of beauty; rends away
All safety from the night, all comfort from the day.

'Then wisely is my soul elate,
    That strife should vanish, battle cease:
I'm poor and of a low estate,
    The mother of the Prince of Peace.
Joy rises in me, like a summer's morn:
Peace, peace on earth! The Prince of Peace is born!'

To God the Son

Great Prince of heaven, begotten of that King
  Who rules the kingdom that Himself did make,
  And of that Virgin Queen man's shape did take,
Which from King David's royal stock did spring!
No marvel, though Thy birth made angels sing,
  And angels' ditties shepherds' pipes awake,
  And kings, like shepherds, humbled for Thy sake,
Kneeled at Thy feet, and gifts of homage bring.
For heaven and earth, the high and low estate,
  As partners of Thy birth, make equal claim:
Angels, because in heaven God Thee begat,
  Shepherds and kings, because Thy mother came
    From princely race, and yet by poverty
    Made glory shine in her humility.

Advent Candle

Commander of wax
Waiting alone
Running from darkness
Chameleon of light
Brightest star
Flame dancer
Most beautiful
Flowing like a wave
The most powerful energy

A Hymn of the Nativity, Sung as by the Shepherds

Chorus: Come, we shepherds, who have seen
Day's king deposed by night's queen:
Come lift we up our lofty song
To wake the sun that sleeps too long.

He, in this our general joy,
   Slept, and dreamt of no such thing,
While we found out the fair-eyed Boy,
   And kissed the cradle of our King.
Tell him he rises now too late
To show us aught worth looking at.

Tell him we now can show him more
Than he e'er showed to mortal sight –
Than he himself e'er saw before,
   Which to be seen needs not his light.
Tell him, Tityrus, where thou hast been:
Tell him, Thyrsis, what thou hast seen.

Tityrus: Gloomy night embraced the place
   Where the noble Infant lay.
The Babe looked up and showed His face;
   In spite of darkness, it was day:
   It was Thy day, sweet, and did rise
Not from the east, but from Thine eyes.

Thyrsis: Winter chid the world, and sent
   The angry north to wage his wars;
The north forgot his fierce intent,
   And left perfumes instead of scars:
By those sweet eyes' persuasive powers,
Where he meant frost he scattered flowers.

Both: We saw Thee in Thy balmy nest,
   Bright Dawn of our eternal day!
We saw Thine eyes break from the east
   And chase the trembling shades away;
We saw Thee, and we blessed the sight;
We saw Thee by Thine own sweet light.

Tityrus: I saw the curled drops, soft and slow,
   Come hovering o'er the place's head,
Offering their whitest sheets of snow
   To furnish the fair Infant's bed.
'Forbear,' said I, 'be not too bold;
Your fleece is white, but 'tis too cold.'

Thyrsis: I saw the officious angels bring
   The down that their soft breasts did strew,
For well they now can spare their wings
   When heaven itself lies here below.
'Fair youth', said I, 'be not too rough,
Thy down, though soft, is not soft enough.'

Tityrus: The Babe no sooner 'gan to seek
   Where to lay His lovely head,
But straight His eyes advised His cheek
   'Twixt mother's breasts to go to bed.
'Sweet choice,' said I; 'no way but so
Not to lie cold, yet sleep in snow.'

All: Welcome to our wondering sight,
   Eternity shut in a span!
Summer in winter, day in night!

Chorus: Heaven in earth and God in man!
Great little One, whose glorious birth
Lifts earth to heaven, stoops heaven to earth!

Welcome, though not to gold nor silk,
　To more than Caesar's birthright is:
Two sister seas of virgin's milk,
　With many a rarely-tempered kiss
That breathes at once both maid and mother,
Warms in the one, cools in the other.

She sings Thy tears asleep and dips
　Her kisses in thy weeping eye;
She spreads the red leaves of Thy lips
　That in their buds yet blushing lie;
She 'gainst those mother-diamonds tries
The points of her young eagle's eyes.

Welcome, though not to those gay flies
　Gilded in the beams of earthly kings –
Slippery souls in smiling eyes;
　But to poor shepherds, simple things,
That use no varnish, no oiled arts,
But lift clean hands full of clear hearts.

Yet when young April's husband-showers
　Shall bless the fruitful Maia's bed,
We'll bring the first-born of her flowers
　To kiss Thy feet and crown Thy head.
To Thee, dread Lamb, whose love must keep
The shepherds more than they the sheep;

To Thee, meek Majesty, soft King
　Of simple graces and sweet loves,
Each of us his lamb will bring,
　Each his pair of silver doves:
At last, in fire of Thy fair eyes,
We'll burn, our own best sacrifice.

'little tree'

little tree
little silent Christmas tree
you are so little
you are more like a flower

who found you in the green forest
and were you very sorry to come away?
see   i will comfort you
because you smell so sweetly

i will kiss your cool bark
and hug you safe and tight
just as your mother would,
only don't be afraid

look   the spangles
that sleep all the year in a dark box
dreaming of being taken out and allowed to shine,
the balls the chains red and gold the fluffy threads,

put up your little arms
and i'll give them all to you to hold
every finger shall have its ring
and there won't be a single place dark or unhappy

then when you're quite dressed
you'll stand in the window for everyone to see
and how they'll stare!
oh but you'll be very proud

and my little sister and i will take hands
and looking up at our beautiful tree
we'll dance and sing
'Noel Noel'

'Eia, Jesus Hodie'

(fifteenth century)

> *Eia, Jesus hodie*
> *Natus est de Virgine.*

Blessed be that maid Mary;
Born He was of her body,
Godès Son that sitteth on high,
  Non ex virile semine.

In a manger of an ass
Jesu lay, and lullayed was,
Hard pains for to pass
  Pro peccante homine.

Kingès came from diverse land
With great giftès in their hand:
In Bethlehem the Child they found,
  Stella ducte lumine.

Man and child, both old and young,
Now in His blissful coming
To that Child mow we sing,
  'Gloria tibi, Domine.'

Noel, noel, in this hall
Make we merry I pray you all;
Unto that Child may we call
  Ullo sine crimine.

A Ballad of Christmas

It was about the deep of night,
  And still was earth and sky,
When in the moonlight, dazzling bright,
  Three ghosts came riding by.

Beyond the sea – beyond the sea,
  Lie kingdoms for them all:
I wot their steeds trod wearily –
  The journey is not small.

By rock and desert, sand and stream,
  They footsore late did go:
Now, like a sweet and blessed dream,
  Their path was deep with snow.

Shining like hoarfrost, rode they on,
  Three ghosts in earth's array:
It was about the hour when wan
  Night turns at hint of day.

Oh, but their hearts with woe distraught
  Hailed not the wane of night,
Only for Jesus still they sought
  To wash them clean and white.

For bloody was each hand, and dark
  With death each orbless eye; –
It was three Traitors mute and stark
  Came riding silent by.

Silver their raiment and their spurs,
  And silver-shod their feet,
And silver-pale each face that stared
  Into the moonlight sweet.

And he upon the left that rode
  Was Pilate, Prince of Rome,
Whose journey once lay far abroad,
  And now was nearing home.

And he upon the right that rode,
  Herod of Salem sate,
Whose mantle dipped in children's blood
  Shone clear as Heaven's gate.

And he, these twain betwixt, that rode
  Was clad as white as wool,
Dyed in the Mercy of his God,
  White was he crown to sole.

Throned mid a myriad Saints in bliss
  Rise shall the Babe of Heaven
To shine on these three ghosts, i-wis,
  Smit through with sorrows seven;

Babe of the Blessed Trinity
  Shall smile their steeds to see:
Herod and Pilate riding by,
  And Judas, one of three.

Nativity

Immensity cloistered in thy dear womb
Now leaves His well-beloved imprisonment,
There He hath made Himself to His intent
Weak enough now into our world to come.
But, oh, for thee, for Him, hath the inn no room?
Yet lay Him in this stall, and from the Orient,
Stars and wise men will travel to prevent
The effect of Herod's jealous general doom.
Seest thou, my soul, with thy faith's eyes, how He
Which fills all place (yet none holds Him) doth lie?
Was not His pity towards thee wondrous high,
That would have need to be pitied by thee?
Kiss Him, and with Him into Egypt go,
With His kind mother, who partakes thy woe.

The Nativity

'Run, shepherds, run where Bethlehem blest appears:
We bring the best of news, be not dismayed:
A Saviour there is born, more old than years,
Amid heaven's rolling heights this earth who stayed.
In a poor cottage inned, a virgin maid
A weakling did Him bear, who all upbears;
This is He, poorly swaddled, in manger laid,
To whom too narrow swaddlings are our spheres.
   Run, shepherds, run, and solemnise His birth:
This is that night – no, day – grown great with bliss,
In which the power of Satan broken is:
In heaven be glory; peace unto the earth.'
  Thus singing through the air the angels swam,
  And cope of stars re-echoed the same.

'Rorate Coeli Desuper'

Rorate coeli desuper.
Heavens, distil your balmy showers,
For now is risen the bright day star
From the rose Mary, flower of flowers:
The clear sun whom no cloud devours,
Surmounting Phoebus in the east,
Is comen of his Heavenly towers,
Et nobis puer natus est.

Archangels, angels, and dominations,
Thrones, potentates, and martyrs seir,
And all ye heavenly operations,
Star, planet, firmament, and sphere,
Fire, earth, air, and water clear,
To Him give loving, most and least,
That came in to so meek manner
Et nobis puer natus est.

Sinners be glad, and penance do,
And thank your Maker heartfully;
For He that ye might not come to
To you is comen full humbly,
Your soulès with His blood to buy
And loose you of the fiend's arrest,
And only of His own mercy:
Pro nobis puer natus est.

All clergy, do to Him incline,
And bow unto that Bairn benign,
And do your observance divine
To Him that is of kingès King:
Incense His altar, read and sing
In holy kirk with mind digest,
Him honouring atour all thing
Qui nobis puer natus est.

Celestial fowlès in the air
Sing with your notès upon height;
In firthès and in forests fair
Be mirthful now at all your might,
For passed is your dully night:
Aurora has the cloudès pierced;
The sun is risen with gladsome light,
Et nobis puer natus est.

Now spring up, flowers, from the root:
Revert you upward naturally,
In honour of the blessed fruit
That rose up from the rose Mary.
Lay out your leavès lustily;
From dead take life now at the least
In worship of that prince worthy
Qui nobis puer natus est.

Sing, heaven imperial, most of height;
Regions of air, make harmony;
All fish in flood, and fowl of flight,
Be mirthful and make melody:
All *Gloria in excelsis* cry,
Heaven, earth, sea, man, bird and beast:
He that is crowned above the sky
Pro nobis puer natus est.

'St Stephen was a Clerk'

(fifteenth century)

Saint Stephen was a clerk
  In King Herod's hall,
And served him of bread and cloth
  As ever king befall.

Stephen out of kitchen came
  With boarès head in hand;
He saw a star was fair and bright
  Over Bethlehem stand.

He cast adown the boarès head
  And went into the hall:
'I forsake thee, King Herod,
  And thy workès all;

'I forsake thee, King Herod,
  And thy workès all:
There is a Child in Bethlem born
  Is better than we all.'

'What aileth thee, Stephen,
  What is thee befall?
Lacketh thee either meat or drink
  In King Herod's hall?'

'Lacketh me neither meat nor drink
  In King Herod's hall:
There is a Child in Bethlem born
  Is better than we all.'

'What aileth thee, Stephen,
  Art thou wode, or thou ginnest to breide?
Lacketh thee either gold or fee
  Or any richè weed?'

'Lacketh me neither gold nor fee,
  Nor none rich weed:
There is a Child in Bethlem born
  Shall helpen us at our need.'

'That is also sooth, Stephen,
  Also sooth, iwis,
As this capon crowè shall
  That lieth here in my dish.'

That word was not so sooner said,
  That word in that hall,
The capon crew *'Christus natus est'*
  Among the lordès all.

'Riseth up, mine tormentors,
  By two and all by one,
And leadeth Stephen out of this town
  And stoneth him with stone.'

Tooken they Stephen
  And stoned him in the way;
And therefore is his even
  On Christès owen day.

from *Christ's Victory in Heaven*

Who can forget – never to be forgot –
The time that all the world in slumber lies,
When, like the stars, the singing angels shot
To earth, and heaven awaked all his eyes
To see another sun at midnight rise
   On earth? Was never sight of pareil fame,
   For God before man like Himself did frame,
But God Himself now like a mortal man became.

A child He was, and had not learnt to speak,
That with His Word the world before did make;
His mother's arms him bore, he was so weak,
That with one hand the vaults of heaven could shake.
See how small room my infant Lord doth take,
   Whom all the world is not enough to hold!
   Who of His years, or of His age, hath told?
Never such age so young, never a child so old.

And yet but newly He was infanted,
And yet already He was sought to die;
Yet scarcely born, already banished;
Not able yet to go, and forced to fly:
But scarcely fled away when, by and by,
   The tyrant's sword with blood is all defiled,
   And Rachel for her sons, with fury wild,
Cried, 'O thou cruel king,' and 'O, my sweetest child!'

Egypt His nurse became, where Nilus springs,
Who straight, to entertain the rising sun,
The hasty harvest in his bosom brings;
But now for drieth the fields were all undone,
And now with waters all is overrun:
   So fast the Cynthian mountains poured their snow,
   When once they felt the sun so near them glow,
That Nilus Egypt lost, and to a sea did grow.

The angels carolled loud their song of peace;
The cursed oracles were stricken dumb;
To see their Shepherd, the poor shepherds press;
To see their King, the kingly sophies come;
And, them to guide unto his Master's home,
  A star comes dancing up the orient,
  That springs for joy over the strawy tent,
Where gold, to make their Prince a crown, they all present.

'There is no Rose'

(fifteenth century)

There is no rose of such virtue
As is the rose that bare Jesu;
   Alleluya.

For in this rose contained was
Heaven and earth in little space,
   Res miranda.

By that rose we may well see
That He is God in persons three,
   Pari forma.

The angels sungen the shepherds to:
'*Gloria in excelsis Deo.*'
   Gaudeamus.

Leave we all this worldly mirth,
And follow we this joyful birth,
   Transeamus.

Hymn

Lord, when the wise men came from far,
Led to Thy cradle by a star,
Then did the shepherds too rejoice,
Instructed by Thy angel's voice:
Blessed were the wise men in their skill,
And shepherds in their harmless will.

Wise men, in tracing nature's laws,
Ascend unto the highest cause;
Shepherds, with humble fearfulness,
Walk safely, though their light be less:
Though wise men better know the way,
It seems no honest heart can stray.

There is no merit in the wise
But love (the shepherds' sacrifice):
Wise men, all ways of knowledge past,
To the shepherds' wonder come at last;
To know can only wonder breed,
And not to know is wonder's seed.

A wise man at the altar bows,
And offers up his studied vows,
And is received. May not the tears,
Which spring too from a shepherd's fears,
And sighs upon his frailty spent
(Though not distinct) be eloquent?

'Tis true, the object sanctifies
All passions which within us rise;
But since no creature comprehends
The cause of causes, end of ends,
He who himself vouchsafes to know
Best pleases his creator so.

When, then, our sorrows we apply
To our own wants and poverty;
When we look up in all distress,
And our own misery confess,
Sending both thanks and prayers above,
Then, though we do not know, we love.

'Noel, Noel, Noel'

(fifteenth century)

'Noel, noel, noel',
Sing we with mirth;
Christ is come well
With us to dwell
By His most noble birth.

Under a tree, in sporting me
Alone by a wood side,
I heard a maid that sweetly said
'I am with child this tide.

'Graciously conceived have I
The Son of God so sweet.
His gracious will I put me till
As mother him to keep.

'Both night and day I will Him pray
And hear his lawès taught,
And every dell His true gospel
In His apostles fraught.

'This ghostly case doth me embrace
Without despite or mock,
With my darling "lullay" to sing
And lovely Him to rock.

'Without distress, in great lightness
I am both night and day:
This heavenly fod in His childhood
Shall daily with me play.

'Soon must I sing with rejoicing,
For the time is all run
That I shall child, all undefiled,
The King of heaven's Son.'

For Christmas Day

Immortal Babe, who this dear day
Didst change Thine heaven for our clay,
And didst with flesh Thy Godhead veil,
Eternal Son of God, all hail!

Shine, happy star! Ye angels, sing
Glory on high to heaven's King!
Run, shepherds, leave your nightly watch,
See heaven come down to Bethlehem's cratch.

Worship, ye sages of the east,
The King of gods in meanness dressed.
O blessed Maid, smile, and adore
The God thy womb and arms hath bore.

Star, angels, shepherds, and wise sages,
Thou virgin glory of all ages,
Restored frame of heaven and earth,
Joy in your dear Redeemer's birth!

The Reminder

While I watch the Christmas blaze
Paint the room with ruddy rays,
Something makes my vision glide
To the frosty scene outside.

There, to reach a rotting berry,
Toils a thrush – constrained to very
Dregs of food by sharp distress,
Taking such with thankfulness.

Why, O starving bird, when I
Our day's joy would justify,
And put misery out of view,
Do you make me notice you!

The Dead Quire

Beside the mead of memories,
Where Church-way mounts to Moaning Hill,
The meek man sighed his phantasies:
      He seems to sigh them still.

'Twas the Birth-tide Eve, and the hamleteers
Made merry with ancient Mellstock zest,
But the Mellstock quire of former years
      Had entered into rest.

'Old Dewy lay by the gaunt yew tree,
And Reuben and Michael a pace behind,
And Bowman with his family
      By the wall that the ivies bind.

'The singers had followed one by one,
Treble, and tenor, and thorough-bass;
And the worm that wasteth had begun
      To mine their mouldering place.

'For two-score years, ere Christ-day light,
Mellstock had throbbed to strains from these;
But now there echoed on the night
      No Christmas harmonies.

'Three meadows off, at a dormered inn,
The youth had gathered in high carouse,
And, ranged on settles, some therein
      Had drunk them to a drowse.

'Loud, lively, reckless, some had grown,
Each dandling on his jigging knee
Eliza, Dolly, Nance, or Joan –
      Livers in levity.

'The taper flames and hearthfire shine
Grew smoke-hazed to a lurid light,
And songs on subjects not divine
    Were warbled forth that night.

'Yet many were sons and grandsons here
Of those who, on such eves gone by,
At that still hour had throated clear
    Their anthems to the sky.

'The clock belled midnight; and ere long
One shouted, "Now 'tis Christmas morn;
Here's to our women, old and young,
    And to John Barleycorn!"

'They drink the toast and shout again:
The pewter-ware rings back the boom,
And for a breath-while follows then
    A silence round the room.

'When nigh without, as in old days,
The ancient quire of voice and string
Seemed singing words of prayer and praise
    As they had used to sing.

'*While shepherds watch'd their flocks by night*, –
Thus swells the long familiar sound
In many a quaint symphonic flight –
    To, *Glory shone around.*

'The sons defined their fathers' tones,
The widow his whom she had wed,
And others in the minor moans
    The viols of the dead.

'Something supernal has the sound
As verse by verse the strain proceeds,
And stilly staring on the ground
    Each roysterer holds and heeds.

'Towards its chorded closing bar
Plaintively, thinly, waned the hymn,
Yet lingered, like the notes afar
    Of banded seraphim.

'With brows abashed, and reverent tread,
The hearkeners sought the tavern door:
But nothing, save wan moonlight, spread
    The empty highway o'er.

'While on their hearing fixed and tense
The aerial music seemed to sink,
As it were gently moving thence
    Along the river brink.

'Then did the Quick pursue the Dead
By crystal Froom that crinkles there;
And still the viewless quire ahead
     Voiced the old holy air.

'By Bank-walk wicket, brightly bleached,
It passed, and 'twixt the hedges twain,
Dogged by the living; till it reached
     The bottom of Church Lane.

'There, at the turning, it was heard
Drawing to where the churchyard lay:
But when they followed thitherward
     It smalled, and died away.

'Each gravestone of the quire, each mound,
Confronted them beneath the moon;
But no more floated therearound
     That ancient Birth-night tune.

'There Dewy lay by the gaunt yew tree,
There Reuben and Michael, a pace behind,
And Bowman with his family
     By the wall that the ivies bind ...

'As from a dream each sobered son
Awoke, and musing reached his door:
'Twas said that of them all, not one
     Sat in a tavern more.'

– The meek man ceased; and ceased to heed
His listener, and crossed the leaze
From Moaning Hill towards the mead –
     The Mead of Memories.

The Oxen

Christmas Eve, and twelve of the clock,
  'Now they are all on their knees,'
An elder said as we sat in a flock
  By the embers in hearthside ease.

We pictured the meek mild creatures where
  They dwelt in their strawy pen,
Nor did it occur to one of us there
  To doubt they were kneeling then.

So fair a fancy few would weave
  In these years! Yet, I feel,
If someone said on Christmas Eve
  'Come; see the oxen kneel

'In the lonely barton by yonder coomb
  Our childhood used to know,'
I should go with him in the gloom,
  Hoping it might be so.

Christmas: 1924

'Peace upon earth!' was said. We sing it,
And pay a million priests to bring it.
After two thousand years of mass
We've got as far as poison gas.

Modryb Marya – Aunt Mary
A Christmas Chant

In old and simple-hearted Cornwall, the household names
'Uncle' and 'Aunt' were uttered and used as they are to this day
in many countries of the East, not only as phrases of kindred,
but as words of kindly greeting and tender respect. It was in the
spirit, therefore, of this touching and graphic usage, that they
were wont on the Tamar side to call the Mother of God in their
loyal language, Modryb Marya, or Aunt Mary.

Now of all the trees by the king's highway,
    Which do you love the best?
Oh! the one that is green upon Christmas Day,
    The bush with the bleeding breast.
Now the holly with her drops of blood for me,
For that is our dear Aunt Mary's tree.

Its leaves are sweet with our Saviour's name,
　'Tis a plant that loves the poor:
Summer and winter it shines the same
　Beside the cottage door.
Oh! the holly with her drops of blood for me,
For that is our Aunt Mary's tree.

'Tis a bush that the birds will never leave:
　They sing on it all day long;
But sweetest of all upon Christmas Eve
　Is heard the robin's song.
'Tis the merriest sound upon earth and sea,
For it comes from our own Aunt Mary's tree.

So, of all that grow by the king's highway,
　I love that tree the best;
'Tis a bower for the birds upon Christmas Day,
　The bush of the bleeding breast.
Oh! the holly with her drops of blood for me,
For that is our sweet Aunt Mary's tree.

The Child Jesus: A Cornish Carol

Welcome that star in Judah's sky,
    That voice o'er Bethlehem's palmy glen:
The lamp far sages hailed on high,
    The tones that thrilled the shepherd men:
Glory to God in loftiest heaven!
    Thus angels smote the echoing chord;
Glad tidings unto man forgiven,
    Peace from the presence of the Lord.

The shepherds sought that birth divine,
    The Wise Men traced their guided way;
There, by strange light and mystic sign,
    The God they came to worship lay.
A human Babe in beauty smiled
    Where lowing oxen round Him trod:
A maiden clasped her awful Child,
    Pure offspring of the breath of God.

Those voices from on high are mute,
    The star the Wise Men saw is dim;
But hope still guides the wanderer's foot,
    And faith renews the angel hymn:
Glory to God in loftiest heaven!
    Touch with glad hand the ancient chord;
Good tidings unto man forgiven,
    Peace from the presence of the Lord.

Christmas Carol

O lovely voices of the sky,
  That hymned the Saviour's birth,
Are ye not singing still on high,
  Ye that sang 'Peace on earth'?
    To us yet speak the strains
      Wherewith, in days gone by,
    Ye blessed the Syrian swains,
      O voices of the sky!

O clear and shining light, whose beams
  That hour heaven's glory shed
Around the palms, and o'er the streams,
  And on the shepherd's head;
    Be near, through life and death,
      As in that holiest night
    Of hope, and joy, and faith,
      O clear and shining light!

O star, which led to Him whose love
  Brought down man's ransom free,
Where art thou? – 'midst the hosts above
  May we still gaze on thee?
    In heaven thou art not set,
      Thy rays earth might not dim –
    Send them to guide us yet,
      O star which led to Him!

Christmas

All after pleasures as I rid one day,
   My horse and I – both tired, body and mind,
   With full cry of affection quite astray –
I took up in the next inn I could find.
There when I came, whom found I but my dear,
   My dearest Lord, expecting till the grief
   Of pleasures brought me to Him, ready there
To be all passengers' most sweet relief?
O Thou, whose glorious, yet contracted, light,
   Wrapped in night's mantle, stole into a manger:
   Since my dark soul and brutish is Thy right,
To man of all beasts be Thou not a stranger:
   Furnish and deck my soul, that Thou mayest have
   A better lodging than a rack or grave.

The shepherds sing, and shall I silent be?
     My God, no hymn for Thee?
My soul's a shepherd, too; a flock it feeds
     Of thoughts, and words, and deeds.
The pasture is Thy word; the streams, Thy grace
     Enriching all the place.
Shepherd and flock shall sing, and all my powers
     Outsing the daylight hours.
Then will we chide the sun for letting night
     Take up his place and right:
We sing one common Lord; wherefore he should
     Himself the candle hold.
I will go searching, till I find a sun
     Shall stay till we have done:
A willing shiner, that shall shine as gladly
     As frost-nipped suns look sadly.
Then we will sing and shine all our own day,
     And one another pay:
His beams shall cheer my breast, and both so twine
Till even his beams sing, and my music shine.

Ceremonies for Christmas

Come, bring with a noise,
My merry, merry boys,
The Christmas log to the firing;
While my good dame, she
Bids ye all be free,
And drink to your heart's desiring.

With the last year's brand
Light the new block, and
For good success in his spending,
On your psalteries play,
That sweet luck may
Come while the log is a-tinding.

Drink now the strong beer,
Cut the white loaf here,
The while the meat is a-shredding;
For the rare mince-pie
And plums stand by
To fill the paste that's a-kneading.

Christmas Eve, another Ceremony

Come guard this night the Christmas pie
That the thief, though ne'er so sly,
With his flesh-hooks don't come nigh
              To catch it.

From him, who all alone sits there,
Having his eyes still in his ear,
And a deal of nightly fear
              To watch it.

A Christmas Carol, Sung to the King in the Presence at Whitehall

Chorus. What sweeter music can we bring,
Than a carol, for to sing
The birth of this, our heavenly King?
Awake the voice! Awake the string!
Heart, ear, and eye, and everything
Awake! the while the active finger
Runs division with the singer.

From the flourish they come to the song

1. Dark and dull night fly hence away,
And give the honour to this day
That sees December turned to May.

2. If we may ask the reason, say
The why and wherefore all things here
Seem like the springtime of the year?

3. Why does the chilling winter's morn
Smile like a field beset with corn,
Or smell like to a mead new-shorn
Thus on the sudden? 4. Come and see
The cause why things thus fragrant be:
'Tis He is born, whose quickening birth
Gives life and lustre, public mirth,
To heaven and the under-earth.

Chorus. We see Him come, and know Him ours,
Who, with His sunshine and His showers
Turns all the patient ground to flowers.

1. The darling of the world is come,
And fit it is we find a room
To welcome Him. 2. The nobler part
Of all the house here, is the heart,

Chorus. Which we will give Him; and bequeath
This holly, and this ivy wreath,
To do Him honour, who's our King,
And Lord of all this revelling.

Twelfth Night, or King and Queen

Now, now the mirth comes
With the cake full of plums,
Where bean's the king of the sport here;
Beside, we must know,
The pea also
Must revel, as queen, in the court here.

Begin then to choose
(This night as ye use)
Who shall for the present delight here:
Be a king by the lot,
And who shall not
Be Twelfth-Day queen for the night here.

Which known, let us make
Joy-sops with the cake,
And let not a man then be seen here
Who, unurged, will not drink
To the base from the brink
A health to the king and queen here.

Next crown the bowl full
With gentle lambs' wool:
Add sugar, nutmeg and ginger,
With store of ale, too.
And thus ye must do
To make the wassail a swinger.

Give then to the king
And queen wassailing;
And though with ale ye be whet here,
Yet part ye from hence
As free from offence
As when ye innocent met here.

'To Bliss God Bring Us'

(fifteenth century)

> To bliss God bring us all and some,
> *Christe redemptor omnium.*

In Bethlehem, that fair city,
Was born a child that was so free,
Lord and Prince of high degree,
Iam lucis orto sidere.

Jesu, for the love of Thee,
Childer were slain great plenty,
In Bethlehem, that fair city,
A solis ortus cardine.

As the sun shineth in the glass,
So Jesu of His mother bornè was.
Him to serve, God give us grace,
O lux beata Trinitas.

Now is He our Lord Jesus;
Thus hath He verily visited us;
Now to make merry among us,
Exultet coelum laudibus.

A Hymn on the Nativity of My Saviour

I sing the birth was born tonight,
The Author both of life and light;
    The angels so did sound it,
And like the ravished shepherds said,
Who saw the light and were afraid,
    Yet searched, and true they found it.

The Son of God, the eternal King,
That did us all salvation bring,
    And freed the soul from danger;
He whom the whole world could not take,
The Word, which heaven and earth did make,
    Was now laid in a manger.

The Father's wisdom willed it so,
The Son's obedience knew no no,
    Both wills were in one stature;
And as that wisdom had decreed,
The Word was now made flesh indeed,
    And took on Him our nature.

What comfort by Him do we win,
Who made Himself the price of sin
    To make us heirs of glory!
To see this Babe, all innocence;
A martyr born in our defence –
    Can man forget this story?

'Alone, Alone, Alone, Alone'

(fifteenth century)

> Alone, alone, alone, alone,
> Here I sit alone, alas, alone!

As I me walked this endris day
To the greenwood for to play
And all heaviness to put away,
> Myself alone;

As I walked under the greenwood bough
I saw a maiden fair enough:
A Child she hoppèd; she sang, she laugh;
> That Child wept alone.

'Son,' she said, 'I have Thee born
To save mankind that was forlorn.
Therefore, I pray Thee, Son, no more,
> But be still alone.'

'Mother, methinketh it is right ill
That men seeketh for to spill;
For them to save, it is My will –
> Therefore I came hither alone.'

'Son,' she said, 'let it be in Thy thought,
For man's guilt is notwithstone;
For thou art He that hath all wrought,
> And I, Thy mother, alone.'

Christmas Day

And suddenly there was with the Angel
a multitude of the heavenly host, praising God.
  – St Luke, ii.13.

What sudden blaze of song
    Spreads o'er the expanse of heaven?
In waves of light it thrills along,
    The angelic signal given –
'Glory to God!' from yonder central fire
Flows out the echoing lay beyond the starry quire;

Like circles widening round
    Upon a clear, blue river,
Orb after orb, the wondrous sound
    Is echoed on for ever;
'Glory to God on high, on earth be peace,
And love towards men of love – salvation and release'.

Yet stay, before thou dare
    To join that festal throng;
Listen and mark what gentle air
    First stirred the tide of song;
'Tis not, 'the Saviour born in David's home,
To whom for power and health obedient worlds should come' –

'Tis not, 'the Christ the Lord'–
    With fixed, adoring look
The choir of angels caught the word,
    Nor yet their silence broke:
But when they heard the sign, where Christ should be,
In sudden light they shone and heavenly harmony.

Wrapped in His swaddling bands,
    And in His manger laid,
The hope and glory of all lands
    Is come to the world's aid:
 No peaceful home upon His cradle smiled,
Guests rudely went and came, where slept the royal child.

But where Thou dwellest, Lord,
    No other thought should be,
Once duly welcomed and adored,
    How should I part with Thee?
 Bethlehem must lose Thee soon, but Thou wilt grace
The single heart to be Thy sure abiding place.

Thee, on the bosom laid
    Of a pure virgin mind,
In quiet ever, and in shade,
    Shepherd and sage may find;
 They, who have bowed untaught to Nature's sway,
And they, who follow Truth along her star-paved way.

The pastoral spirits first
    Approach Thee, Babe divine,
For they in lowly thoughts are nursed,
    Meet for Thy lowly shrine.
 Sooner than they should miss where Thou dost dwell,
Angels from heaven will stoop to guide them to Thy cell.

Still, as the day comes round
    For Thee to be revealed,
By wakeful shepherds Thou art found,
    Abiding in the field.
 All through the wintry heaven and chill night air
In music and in light Thou dawnest on their prayer.

O faint ye not for fear –
What though your wandering sheep,
Reckless of what they see and hear,
Lie lost in wilful sleep?
High heaven in mercy to your sad annoy
Still greets you with glad tidings of immortal joy.

Think on the eternal home
The Saviour left for you;
Think on the Lord most holy, come
To dwell with hearts untrue:
So shall ye tread untired his pastoral ways,
And in the darkness sing your carol of high praise.

For Christmas Day

Rejoice, rejoice, with heart and voice!
In Christè's birth this day rejoice!
From virgin's womb this day did spring
The precious seed that only saved man.
This day let man rejoice and sweetly sing,
Since on this day salvation first began.
   This day did Christ man's soul from death remove,
   With glorious saints to dwell in heaven above.

This day to man came pledge of perfect peace;
This day to man came perfect unity;
This day man's grief began for to surcease;
This day did man receive a remedy
   For each offence and every deadly sin
   With guilty heart that erst he wandered in.

In Christè's flock let love be surely placed;
From Christè's flock let concord hate expel;
Of Christè's flock let love be so embraced
As we in Christ and Christ in us may dwell:
   Christ is the author of all unity,
   From whence proceedeth all felicity.

Oh sing unto this glittering, glorious King;
Oh praise His name let every living thing;
Let heart and voice, like bells of silver, ring
The comfort that this day doth bring:
   Let lute, let shawm, with sound of sweet delight,
   The joy of Christè's birth this day recite.

'Ah, My Dear, Ah, My Dear Son'

(fifteenth century)

'Ah, my dear, ah, my dear Son,'
   Said Mary, 'Ah, my dear.
Kiss thy mother, Jesu,
   With a laughing cheer.'

This endris night
I saw a sight
   All in my sleep:
Mary, that may,
She sang lullay
   And sore did weep.
To keep she sought
Full fast above
   Her Son from cold;
Joseph said, 'Wife,
My joy, my life,
   Say what ye wolde.'
'Nothing, my spouse,
Is in this house
   Unto my pay:
My Son – a King
That made all thing –
   Lieth in hay.'

'My mother dear,
Amend your cheer,
  And now be still.
Thus for to lie,
It is soothly
  My Father's will.
Derision,
Great passion
  Infinitely, infinitely,
As it is found,
Many a wound,
  Suffer shall I.
On Calvary,
That is so high,
  There shall I be,
Man to restore,
Nailed full sore
  Upon a tree.'

Christmas Landscape

Tonight the wind gnaws
with teeth of glass,
the jackdaw shivers
in caged branches of iron,
the stars have talons.

There is hunger in the mouth
of vole and badger,
silver agonies of breath
in the nostril of the fox,
ice on the rabbit's paw.

Tonight has no moon,
no food for the pilgrim;
the fruit tree is bare,
the rose bush a thorn
and the ground is bitter with stones.

But the mole sleeps, and the hedgehog
lies curled in a womb of leaves,
the bean and the wheat-seed
hug their germs in the earth
and the stream moves under the ice.

Tonight there is no moon,
but a new star opens
like a silver trumpet over the dead.
Tonight in a nest of ruins
the blessèd babe is laid.

And the fir tree warms to a bloom of candles,
the child lights his lantern,
stares at his tinselled toy;
our hearts and hearths
smoulder with live ashes.

In the blood of our grief
the cold earth is suckled,
in our agony the womb
convulses its seed,
in the cry of anguish
the child's first breath is born.

'Nay, Ivy, Nay, It Shall Not Be, Iwis'
(fifteenth century)

> Nay, Ivy, nay, it shall not be, iwis,
> Let Holly have the mastery, as the manner is.

Holly stand in the hall, fair to behold;
Ivy stand without the door: she is full sore a-cold.

Holly and his merry men, they dancen and they sing;
Ivy and her maidens, they weepen and they wring.

Ivy hath a kibe: she caught it with the cold;
So mote they all have each that with Ivy hold.

Holly hath berries as red as any rose;
The forester and the hunters keep them from the does.

Ivy hath berries as black as any sloe;
There come the owl and eat him as she go.

Holly hath birdès, a full fair flock,
The nightingale, the popinjay, the gentle laverock.

Good Ivy, what birdès hast thou?
None but the owlet, that cries 'how, how'.

> Nay, Ivy, nay, it shall not be, iwis;
> Let Holly have the mastery, as the manner is.

The Glastonbury Thorn

There grew, within a favoured vale,
As old traditions tell the tale,
A famous, flowering, Eastern thorn,
Which blossom'd every Christmas morn.

No lowly hearth, no lordly hall,
New dress'd for the yearly festival,
But gathered it, as the gift of May,
To honour the auspicious day.

And brightly mid the Christmas green
It shines, in the fire-light's ruddy sheen,
Mix'd with hard berries that gleam and glow
From holly and from mistletoe.

That tree is like the Tree of Life,
Which buds when the season of joy is rife,
And flowers when the bright dawn wakes above
The day that Religion gave birth to Love.

And, as Time the eternal morn resumes,
Humanity's grateful joy o'erblooms
The naked sight of the bleeding thorn,
Which Love on his brows for man hath worn.

O! let us still through love unite
To celebrate the holy rite;
That all the thorns of life may show
Nought but sweet flowers above the snow!

Christmas 1970

A little girl called Silé Javotte
Said 'Look at the lovely presents I've got'
While a little girl in Biafra said
'Oh what a lovely slice of bread.'

On the Morning of Christ's Nativity

Composed 1629

This is the month, and this the happy morn
Wherein the Son of heaven's eternal King,
Of wedded maid and virgin mother born,
Our great redemption from above did bring;
For so the holy sages once did sing,
   That He our deadly forfeit should release,
And with His Father work us a perpetual peace.

That glorious form, that light unsufferable,
And that far-beaming blaze of majesty,
Wherewith He wont at heaven's high council-table
To sit the midst of trinal unity,
He laid aside; and here with us to be,
   Forsook the courts of everlasting day,
And chose with us a darksome house of mortal clay.

Say, heavenly muse, shall not thy sacred vein
Afford a present to the Infant God?
Hast thou no verse, no hymn or solemn strain,
To welcome Him to this His new abode,
Now while the heaven, by the sun's team untrod,
   Hath took no print of the approaching light,
And all the spangled host keep watch in squadrons bright?

See how from far upon the eastern road
The star-led wizards haste with odours sweet!
O run! Prevent them with thy humble ode,
And lay it lowly at His blessed feet.
Have thou the honour first thy Lord to greet,
   And join thy voice unto the angel quire,
From out His secret altar touched with hallowed fire.

The Hymn

It was the winter wild,
While the heaven-born Child
   All meanly wrapped in the rude manger lies;
Nature in awe to Him
Had doffed her gaudy trim,
   With her great Master so to sympathise:
It was no season then for her
To wanton with the sun, her lusty paramour.

Only with speeches fair
She woos the gentle air
   To hide her guilty front with innocent snow,
And on her naked shame
(Pollute with sinful blame)
   The saintly veil of maiden white to throw –
Confounded that her Maker's eyes
Should look so near upon her foul deformities.

But He, her fears to cease,
Sent down the meek-eyed Peace:
   She, crowned with olive green, came softly sliding
Down through the turning sphere,
His ready harbinger,
   With turtle wing the amorous clouds dividing;
And, waving wide her myrtle wand,
She strikes a universal peace through sea and land.

Nor war or battle's sound
Was heard the world around,
   The idle spear and shield were high up-hung;
The hooked chariot stood
Unstained with hostile blood;
   The trumpet spake not to the armed throng;
And kings sat still with awful eye,
As if they surely knew their sovereign Lord was by.

But peaceful was the night
Wherein the Prince of Light
    His reign of peace upon the earth began:
The winds with wonder whist,
Smoothly the waters kissed,
    Whispering new joys to the mild ocean,
Who now hath quite forgot to rave,
While birds of calm sit brooding on the charmed wave.

The stars with deep amaze
Stand fixed in steadfast gaze,
    Bending one way their precious influence,
And will not take their flight –
For all the morning light,
    Or Lucifer, that often warned them thence –
But in their glimmering orbs did glow
Until their Lord Himself bespake, and bid them go.

And though the shady gloom
Had given day her room,
    The sun himself withheld his wonted speed,
And hid his head for shame
As his inferior flame
    The new-enlightened world no more should need:
He saw a greater Sun appear
Than his bright throne or burning axle-tree could bear.

The shepherds on the lawn,
Or ere the point of dawn,
    Sat simply chatting in a rustic row;
Full little thought they then
That the mighty Pan
    Was kindly come to live with them below.
Perhaps their loves, or else their sheep,
Was all that did their silly thoughts so busy keep:

When such music sweet
Their hearts and ears did greet,
   As never was by mortal finger strook –
Divinely-warbled voice
Answering the stringed noise,
   As all their souls in blissful rapture took;
The air, such pleasure loath to lose,
With thousand echoes still prolongs each heavenly close.

Nature – that heard such sound
Beneath the hollow round
   Of Cynthia's seat the airy region thrilling –
Now was almost won
To think her part was done,
   And that her reign had here its last fulfilling:
She knew such harmony alone
Could hold all heaven and earth in happier union.

At last surrounds their sight
A globe of circular light
   That with long beams the shame-faced night arrayed;
The helmed cherubim,
And sworded seraphim,
   Are seen in glittering ranks with wings displayed,
Harping in loud and solemn quire
With unexpressive notes to heaven's new-born heir.

Such music (as 'tis said)
Before was never made
   But when, of old, the sons of morning sung
While the Creator great
His constellations set,
   And the well-balanced world on hinges hung,
And cast the dark foundations deep,
And bid the weltering waves their oozy channel keep.

Ring out, ye crystal spheres,
Once bless our human ears
   (If ye have power to touch our senses so),
And let your silver chime
Move in melodious time;
   And let the bass of heaven's deep organ blow,
And with your ninefold harmony
Make up full consort to the angelic symphony.

For if such holy song
Enwrap our fancy long,
   Time will run back and fetch the age of gold,
And speckled Vanity
Will sicken and soon die,
   And leprous Sin will melt from earthly mould,
And Hell itself will pass away
And leave her dolorous mansions to the peering day.

Yea, Truth and Justice then
Will down return to men,
   Orbed in a rainbow; and, like glories wearing,
Mercy will sit between
Throned in celestial sheen,
   With radiant feet the tissued clouds down steering;
And heaven, as at some festival,
Will open wide the gates of her high palace hall.

But wisest Fate says No,
This must not yet be so:
   The Babe lies yet in smiling infancy
That on the bitter cross
Must redeem our loss,
   So both Himself and us to glorify:
Yet first to those ychained in sleep
The wakeful trump of doom must thunder through the deep,

With such a horrid clang
As on Mount Sinai rang
 While the red fire and smouldering clouds outbreak:
The aged earth, aghast
With terror of that blast,
 Shall from the surface to the centre shake
When, at the world's last session,
The dreadful Judge in middle air shall spread His throne.

And then at last our bliss
Full and perfect is,
 But now begins; for from this happy day
The old dragon under ground,
In straiter limits bound,
 Not half so far casts his usurped sway,
And, wroth to see his kingdom fail,
Swinges the scaly horror of his folded tail.

The oracles are dumb:
No voice or hideous hum
 Runs through the arched roof in words deceiving.
Apollo from his shrine
Can no more divine,
 With hollow shriek the steep of Delphos leaving.
No nightly trance or breathed spell
Inspires the pale-eyed priest from the prophetic cell.

The lonely mountains o'er,
And the resounding shore,
 A voice of weeping heard and loud lament;
From haunted spring and dale
Edged with poplar pale,
 The parting genius is with sighing sent;
With flower-inwoven tresses torn
The nymphs in twilight shade of tangled thickets mourn.

In consecrated earth,
And on the holy hearth,
   The lars and lemures moan with midnight plaint;
In urns and dying altars round
A drear and dying sound
   Affrights the flamens at their service quaint;
And the chill marble seems to sweat
While each peculiar power forgoes his wonted seat.

Peor and Baalim
Forsake their temples dim,
   With that twice-battered god of Palestine;
And mooned Ashtaroth,
Heaven's queen and mother both,
   Now sit not girt with tapers' holy shine;
The Libyc Hammon shrinks his horn;
In vain the Tyrian maids their wonted Thammuz mourn.

And sullen Moloch, fled,
Hath left in shadows dread
   His burning idol all of blackest hue;
In vain with cymbals' ring
They call the grisly king
   In dismal dance about the furnace blue.
The brutish gods of Nile as fast,
Isis and Orus and the dog Anubis, haste.

Nor is Osiris seen
In Memphian grove or green,
   Trampling the unshowered grass with lowings loud;
Nor can he be at rest
Within his sacred chest:
   Naught but profoundest hell can be his shroud.
In vain with timbrelled anthems dark
The sable-stoled sorcerers bear his worshipped ark:

He feels from Judah's land
The dreaded Infant's hand;
   The rays of Bethlehem blind his dusky eyen.
Nor all the gods beside
Longer dare abide,
   Not Typhon huge, ending in snaky twine:
Our Babe, to show His Godhead true,
Can in His swaddling bands control the damned crew.

So, when the sun in bed,
Curtained in cloudy red,
   Pillows his chin upon an orient wave,
The flocking shadows pale
Troop to the infernal jail;
   Each fettered ghost slips to his several grave,
And the yellow-skirted fays
Fly after the night steeds, leaving their moon-loved maze.

But see, the virgin blest
Hath laid her Babe to rest:
   Time is our tedious song should here have ending.
Heaven's youngest-teemed star
Hath fixed her polished car,
   Her sleeping Lord with handmaid lamp attending;
And all about the courtly stable
Bright-harnessed angels sit in order serviceable.

A Visit from St Nicholas

'Twas the night before Christmas, when all through the house
Not a creature was stirring, not even a mouse;
The stockings were hung by the chimney with care,
In hopes that St Nicholas soon would be there;
The children were nestled all snug in their beds,
While visions of sugar-plums danced in their heads;
And mamma in her 'kerchief, and I in my cap,
Had just settled our brains for a long winter's nap,
When out on the lawn there arose such a clatter,
I sprang from the bed to see what was the matter.
Away to the window I flew like a flash,
Tore open the shutters and threw up the sash.
The moon on the breast of the new-fallen snow
Gave the lustre of mid-day to objects below,
When, what to my wondering eyes should appear,
But a miniature sleigh, and eight tiny reindeer,
With a little old driver, so lively and quick,
I knew in a moment it must be St Nick.
More rapid than eagles his coursers they came,
And he whistled, and shouted, and called them by name,
'Now Dasher! now, Dancer! now, Prancer and Vixen!
On, Comet! on, Cupid! on, Donner and Blitzen!
To the top of the porch! to the top of the wall!
Now dash away! dash away! dash away all!'
As dry leaves that before the wild hurricane fly,
When they meet with an obstacle, mount to the sky,
So up to the house-top the coursers they flew,
With the sleigh full of toys, and St Nicholas too.
And then, in a twinkling, I heard on the roof
The prancing and pawing of each little hoof.
As I drew in my head, and was turning around,
Down the chimney St Nicholas came with a bound.

He was dressed all in fur from his head to his foot,
And his clothes were all tarnished with ashes and soot.
A bundle of toys he had flung on his back,
And he looked like a pedlar, just opening his pack.
His eyes – how they twinkled! his dimples – how merry!
His cheeks were like roses, his nose like a cherry!
His droll little mouth was drawn up like a bow,
And the beard of his chin was as white as the snow;
The stump of a pipe he held tight in his teeth,
And the smoke it encircled his head like a wreath;
He had a broad face and a little round belly,
That shook when he laughed, like a bowlful of jelly.
He was chubby and plump, a right jolly old elf,
And I laughed when I saw him in spite of myself;
A wink of his eye and a twist of his head,
Soon gave me to know I had nothing to dread.
He spoke not a word, but went straight to his work,
And filled all the stockings, then turned with a jerk,
And laying his finger aside of his nose,
And giving a nod, up the chimney he rose;
He sprang to his sleigh, to his team gave a whistle,
And away they all flew like the down of a thistle.
But I heard him exclaim, ere he drove out of sight,
'Happy Christmas to all, and to all a good-night!'

'Outlanders, Whence Come Ye Last?'
from *The Earthly Paradise*, September

Outlanders, whence come ye last?
The snow in the street and the wind on the door.
Through what green seas and great have ye passed?
Minstrels and maids, stand forth on the floor.

From far away, O masters mine,
The snow in the street and the wind on the door.
We come to bear you goodly wine:
Minstrels and maids, stand forth on the floor.

From far away we come to you,
The snow in the street and the wind on the door.
To tell of great tidings strange and true:
Minstrels and maids, stand forth on the floor.

News, news of the Trinity,
The snow in the street and the wind on the door.
And Mary and Joseph from over the sea:
Minstrels and maids, stand forth on the floor.

For as we wandered far and wide,
The snow in the street and the wind on the door.
What hap do ye deem there should us betide?
Minstrels and maids, stand forth on the floor.

Under a bent when the night was deep,
The snow in the street and the wind on the door.
There lay three shepherds tending their sheep:
Minstrels and maids, stand forth on the floor.

'O, ye shepherds, what have ye seen,
The snow in the street and the wind on the door.
To slay your sorrow and heal your teen?'
Minstrels and maids, stand forth on the floor.

'In an ox-stall this night we saw,
  The snow in the street and the wind on the door.
A Babe and a maid without a flaw.
  Minstrels and maids, stand forth on the floor.

'There was an old man there beside,
  The snow in the street and the wind on the door.
His hair was white, and his hood was wide.
  Minstrels and maids, stand forth on the floor.

'And as we gazed this thing upon,
  The snow in the street and the wind on the door.
Those twain knelt down to the Little One.
  Minstrels and maids, stand forth on the floor.

'And a marvellous song we straight did hear,
  The snow in the street and the wind on the door.
That slew our sorrows and healed our care.'
  Minstrels and maids, stand forth on the floor.

News of a fair and marvellous thing,
  The snow in the street and the wind on the door,
Nowell, nowell, nowell, we sing!
  Minstrels and maids, stand forth on the floor.

'Be Merry, all that be Present'

(sixteenth century)

Be merry, all that be present:
Omnes de Saba venient.

Out of the east a star shone bright
For to show three kingès light,
Which had far travelled by day and night
    To seek that Lord that all hath sent.

Thereof King Herod heard anon,
That three kings should come through his region
To seek a Child that peer had none,
    And after them soon he sent.

King Herod cried to them on high,
'Ye go to seek a Child truly:
Go forth, and come again me by
    And tell me where that He is lent.'

Forth they went by the starrès leam,
Till they came to merry Bethlehem.
There they found that sweet Bairn-team
    That sith for us His blood hath spent.

Balthazar kneeled first adown,
And said: 'Hail, King of most renown!
And of all kings thou bear'st the crown;
    Therefore with gold I Thee present.'

Melchior kneeled down in that stead,
And said: 'Hail, Lord, in Thy priesthood,
Receive incense to Thy manhood:
    I bring it with a good intent.'

Caspar kneeled down in that stead,
And said: 'Hail, Lord, in Thy knighthood!
I offer Thee myrrh to Thy Godhead,
   For Thou art He that all hath sent.'

Now lords and ladies in rich array,
Lift up your hearts upon this day
And ever to God let us pray,
   That on the rood was rent.

Carol

Mary laid her Child among
  The bracken-fronds of night –
And by the glimmer round His head
  All the barn was lit.

Mary held her Child above
  The miry, frozen farm –
And by the fire within His limbs
  The resting roots were warm.

Mary hid her Child between
  Hillocks of hard sand –
By singing water in His veins
  Grass sprang from the ground.

Mary nursed her Child beside
  The gardens of a grave –
And by the death within His bones
  The dead became alive.

'Nova, Nova, "Ave" Fit ex "Eva"'

(sixteenth century)

> *Nova, nova:*
> *'Ave' fit ex 'Eva'.*

Gabriel of high degree,
He came down from the Trinity,
From Nazareth to Galilee,
    With *nova.*

He met a maiden in a place;
He kneeled down before her face;
He said: 'Hail, Mary, full of grace.'
    With *nova.*

When the maiden saw all this,
She was sore abashed, iwis,
Lest that she had done amiss;
    With *nova.*

Then said the angel: 'Dread not you;
Ye shall conceive in all virtue
A Child whose name shall be Jesu.'
    With *nova.*

Then said the maid: 'How may this be,
Godès Son born of me?
I know not of man's carnality.'
    With *nova.*

Then said the angel anon right:
'The Holy Ghost is on the plight;
There is nothing impossible to God Almight.'
   With *nova.*

Then said the angel anon:
'It is not fully six month agone
Since Saint Elizabeth conceived St John.'
   With *nova.*

Then said the maid anon a-high:
'I am God's own truly:
Ecce ancilla Domini.'
   With *nova.*

On Christmas Day: To My Heart

Today,
Hark! Heaven sings;
Stretch, tune, my heart!
(For hearts have strings
May bear their part)
And though thy lute were bruised i' the Fall,
Bruised hearts may teach an humble pastoral.

Today,
Shepherds rejoice,
And angels do
No more: thy voice
Can reach that too:
Bring then at least thy pipe along
And mingle consort with the angels' song.

Today,
A shed that's thatched
(Yet straws can sing)
Holds God; God matched
With beasts; beasts bring
Their song their way: for shame, then, raise
Thy notes! Lambs bleat, and oxen bellow praise.

Today,
God honoured man
Not angels: yet
They sing; and can
Raised man forget?
Praise is our debt today; now shall
Angels (man's not so poor) discharge it all?

Today,
Then, screw thee high,
My heart, up to
The angels' key;
Sing 'Glory', do:
What if thy strings all crack and fly?
On such a ground, music 'twill be to die.

Regina Coeli

Say, did his sisters wonder what could Joseph see
In a mild, silent little Maid like thee?
And was it awful, in that narrow house,
With God for Babe and Spouse?
Nay, like thy simple, female sort, each one
Apt to find Him in Husband and in Son,
Nothing to thee came strange in this.
Thy wonder was but wondrous bliss:
Wondrous, for, though
True Virgin lives but does not know,
(Howbeit none ever yet confess'd,)
That God lies really in her breast,
Of thine He made His special nest!
And so
All mothers worship little feet,
And kiss the very ground they've trod;
But, ah, thy little Baby sweet
Who was indeed thy God!

'The Boar's Head in Hand Bring I'

(sixteenth century)

> *Caput apri defero,*
> *Reddens laudes Domino.*

The boar's head in hand bring I,
With garlands gay and rosemary;
I pray you all, sing merrily,
  Qui estis in convivio.

The boar's head, I understand,
Is the chief service in this land:
Look, wherever it be found,
  Servite cum cantico.

Be glad, lords, both more and less,
  For this hath ordained our steward
To cheer you all this Christmas,
  The boar's head with mustard.

On the Infancy of Our Saviour

Hail, blessed Virgin, full of heavenly grace,
Blest above all that sprang from human race;
Whose heaven-saluted womb brought forth in one
A blessed Saviour and a blessed Son.
Oh, what a ravishment it had been to see
Thy little Saviour perking on thy knee!
To see Him nuzzle in thy virgin-breast,
His milk-white body all unclad, undressed!
To see thy busy fingers clothe and wrap
His spreading limbs in thy indulgent lap!
To see His desperate eyes with childish grace
Smiling upon His smiling mother's face!
And when His forward strength began to bloom,
To see Him diddle up and down the room!
Oh, who would think so sweet a Babe as this
Should e'er be slain by a false-hearted kiss!
Had I a rag, if, sure, Thy body wore it,
Pardon, sweet Babe, I think I should adore it!
Till then, O grant this boon (a boon, or dearer),
The weed not being, I may adore the wearer.

Born in Winter

Phlegmatic winter on a bed of snow
Lay spitting full of rheum: the sun was now
Inned at the Goat; the melancholic earth
Had her womb bound, and, hopeless of the birth
Of one poor flower, the fields, wood, meads, and all
Feared in this snowy sheet a funeral.
Nor only senseless plants were in decay:
Man, who's a plant reversed, was worse than they.
He had a spiritual winter, and bereft
Not of his leaves, but juice – nay, nothing less –
His passive power to live was so abated
He was not to be raised, but new created.
When all things else were perished, and when
No flowers were but in their causes, then
This wondrous flower itself to act did bring,
And winter was the flower of Jesse's spring.

'My Sweet Little Baby...'

(published 1588)

My sweet little Baby, what meanest Thou to cry?
Be still, my blessed Babe, though cause Thou hast to mourn,
Whose blood most innocent to shed the cruel king hath sworn;
And lo, alas! behold what slaughter he doth make,
Shedding the blood of infants all, sweet Saviour, for Thy sake.
A King, a King is born, they say, which King this king would kill:
O woe, and woeful heavy day, when wretches have their will!
                    Lulla, la lulla, lulla lullaby.

Three kings this King of kings to see are come from far,
To each unknown, with offerings great, by guiding of a star;
And shepherds heard the song which angels bright did sing,
Giving all glory unto God for coming of this King,
Which must be made away – King Herod would Him kill:
O woe, and woeful heavy day, when wretches have their will!
                    Lulla, la lulla, lulla lullaby.

Lo, lo, my little Babe, be still, lament no more;
From fury Thou shalt step aside, help have we still in store:
We heavenly warning have some other soil to seek;
From death must fly the Lord of life, as lamb both mild and
 meek:
Thus must my Babe obey the king that would Him kill;
O woe, and woeful heavy day, when wretches have their will!
                    Lulla, la lulla, lulla lullaby.

But Thou shalt live and reign, as sibyls hath foresaid,
As all the prophets prophecy, whose mother, yet a maid
And perfect virgin pure, with her breasts shall upbreed
Both God and man that all hath made, the Son of heavenly seed:
Whom caitiffs none can 'tray, whom tyrants none can kill:
O joy, and joyful happy day, when wretches want their will!
                    Lulla, la lulla, lulla lullaby.

Advent

The Advent moon shines cold and clear,
   These Advent nights are long;
Our lamps have burned year after year
   And still their flame is strong.

'Watchman, what of the night?' we cry
   Heart-sick with hope deferred:
'No speaking signs are in the sky,'
   Is still the watchman's word.

The Porter watches at the gate,
   The servants watch within;
The watch is long betimes and late,
   The prize is slow to win.

'Watchman, what of the night?' but still
   His answer sounds the same:
'No daybreak tops the utmost hill,
   Nor pale our lamps of flame.'

One to another hear them speak
  The patient virgins wise:
'Surely He is not far to seek' –
  'All night we watch and rise.'

'The days are evil looking back,
  The coming days are dim;
Yet count we not His promise slack,
  But watch and wait for Him.'

One with another, soul with soul,
  They kindle fire from fire:
'Friends watch us who have touched the goal.'
  'They urge us come up higher.'

'With them we shall rest our waysore feet,
  With them is built our home,
With Christ.' – 'They sweet, but He most sweet,
  Sweeter than honeycomb.'

There no more parting, no more pain,
  The distant ones brought near,
The lost so long are found again,
  Long lost but longer dear:

Eye hath not seen, ear hath not heard,
  Nor heart conceived that rest,
With them our good things long deferred,
  With Jesus Christ our Best.

We weep because the night is long,
  We laugh for day shall rise,
We sing a slow contented song
  And knock at Paradise.

Weeping we hold Him fast, Who wept
    For us, we hold Him fast;
And will not let Him go except
    He bless us first or last.

Weeping we hold Him fast tonight;
    We will not let Him go
Till daybreak smite our wearied sight
    And summer smite the snow:

Then figs shall bud, and dove with dove
    Shall coo the livelong day;
Then He shall say, 'Arise, My love,
    My fair one, come away.'

A Christmas Carol

In the bleak mid-winter
  Frosty wind made moan,
Earth stood hard as iron,
  Water like a stone;
Snow had fallen, snow on snow,
  Snow on snow,
In the bleak mid-winter,
  Long ago.

Our God, Heaven cannot hold Him
  Nor earth sustain;
Heaven and earth shall flee away
  When He comes to reign:
In the bleak mid-winter
  A stable-place sufficed
The Lord God Almighty
  Jesus Christ.

Enough for Him whom cherubim
  Worship night and day,
A breastful of milk
  And a mangerful of hay;
Enough for Him whom angels
  Fall down before,
The ox and ass and camel
  Which adore.

Angels and archangels
  May have gathered there,
Cherubim and seraphim
  Throng'd the air,
But only His mother
  In her maiden bliss
Worshipped the Beloved
  With a kiss.

What can I give Him,
  Poor as I am?
If I were a shepherd
  I would bring a lamb,
If I were a wise man
  I would do my part, –
Yet what I can I give Him,
  Give my heart.

'Listen to me, and you shall hear...'

(published 1646)

Listen to me, and you shall hear
News hath not been this thousand year:
Since Herod, Caesar, and many more,
You never heard the like before.
  Holidays are despised,
  New fashions are devised,
Old Christmas is kicked out of town.
  Yet let's be content,
  And the times lament,
You see the world turned upside down.

The wise men did rejoice to see
Our Saviour Christ's nativity:
The angels did good tidings bring,
The shepherds did rejoice and sing.
  Let all honest men
  Take example by them.
Why should we from good laws be bound?
  Yet let's be content,
  And the times lament,
You see the world turned upside down.

Command is given, we must obey,
And quite forget old Christmas day:
Kill a thousand men, or a town regain,
We will give thanks and praise amain.
  The wine pot shall clink,
  We will feast and drink,
And then strange notions will abound.
  Yet let's be content,
  And the times lament,
You see the world turned upside down.

Our lords and knights, and gentry too,
Do mean old fashions to forgo:
They set a porter at the gate,
That none may enter in thereat.
   They count it a sin
   When poor people come in:
Hospitality itself is drowned.
   Yet let's be content,
   And the times lament,
You see the world turned upside down.

The serving men do sit and whine,
And think it long ere dinner time:
The butler's still out of the way,
Or else my lady keeps the key;
   The poor old cook
   In the larder doth look,
Where is no goodness to be found.
   Yet let's be content,
   And the times lament,
You see the world turned upside down.

To conclude, I'll tell you news that's right:
Christmas was killed at Naseby fight;
Charity was slain at the same time,
Jack Tell-Troth, too, a friend of mine.
   Likewise then did die
   Roast beef and shred pie;
Pig, goose, and capon in no quarter found.
   Yet let's be content,
   And the times lament,
You see the world turned upside down.

from *Marmion*

Heap on more wood! – the wind is chill;
But let it whistle as it will,
We'll keep our Christmas merry still.
Each age has deemed the new-born year
The fittest time for festal cheer ...

And well our Christian sires of old
Loved when the year its course had rolled,
And brought blithe Christmas back again,
With all his hospitable train.
Domestic and religious rite
Gave honour to the holy night:
On Christmas Eve the bells were rung;
On Christmas Eve the mass was sung:
That only night of all the year
Saw the stoled priest the chalice rear.
The damsel donned her kirtle sheen;
The hall was dressed with holly green;
Forth to the wood did merry-men go,
To gather in the mistletoe.
Then opened wide the baron's hall
To vassal, tenant, serf and all;
Power laid his rod of rule aside,
And Ceremony doffed his pride.

The heir, with roses in his shoes,
That night might village partner choose;
The lord, underogating, share
The vulgar game of 'post and pair'.
All hailed, with uncontrolled delight
And general voice, the happy night
That, to the cottage, as the crown,
Brought tidings of salvation down.

The fire, with well-dried logs supplied,
Went roaring up the chimney wide;
The huge hall-table's oaken face,
Scrubbed till it shone, the day to grace,
Bore then upon its massive board
No mark to part the squire and lord.
Then was brought in the lusty brawn
By old, blue-coated serving man;
Then the grim boar's head frowned on high,
Crested with bays and rosemary.
Well can the green-garbed ranger tell
How, when, and where, the monster fell;
What dogs before his death he tore,
And all the baiting of the boar.
The wassail round, in good brown bowls,
Garnished with ribbons, blithely trowls.
There the huge sirloin reeked; hard by
Plum-porridge stood, and Christmas pie;
Nor failed old Scotland to produce,
At such high tide, her savoury goose.
Then came the merry maskers in,
And carols roared with blithesome din;
If unmelodious was the song,
It was a hearty note, and strong.

Who lists may in their mumming see
Traces of ancient mystery;
White shirts supplied the masquerade,
And smutted cheeks the visors made.
But oh, what maskers, richly dight,
Can boast of bosoms half so light!
England was merry England when
Old Christmas brought his sports again.
'Twas Christmas broached the mightiest ale;
'Twas Christmas told the merriest tale;
A Christmas gambol oft could cheer
The poor man's heart through half the year …

from *Hamlet*

Barnardo: [The ghost] was about to speak when the cock crew.
Horatio: And then it started up like a guilty thing
 Upon a fearful summons. I have heard
 The cock, that is the trumpet to the morn,
 Doth with his lofty and shrill-sounding throat
 Awake the god of day, and at his warning,
 Whether in sea or fire, in earth or air,
 Th' extravagant and erring spirit hies
 To his confine; and of the truth herein
 This present object made probation.
Marcellus: It faded on the crowing of the cock.
 Some say that, ever 'gainst that season comes
 Wherein our Saviour's birth is celebrated,
 This bird of dawning singeth all night long:
 And then, they say, no spirit dare stir abroad,
 The nights are wholesome, then no planets strike,
 No fairy takes, nor witch hath power to charm,
 So hallowed and so gracious is that time.

In the Workhouse

It is Christmas Day in the workhouse,
    And the cold bare walls are bright
With garlands of green and holly,
    And the place is a pleasant sight:
For with clean-washed hands and faces,
    In a long and hungry line
The paupers sit at the tables,
    For this is the hour they dine.

And the guardians and their ladies,
    Although the wind is east,
Have come in their furs and wrappers,
    To watch their charges feast;
To smile and be condescending,
    Put pudding on pauper plates,
To be hosts at the workhouse banquet
    They've paid for – with the rates.

Oh, the paupers are meek and lowly
    With their 'Thank'ee kindly, mum's';
So long as they fill their stomachs,
    What matter it whence it comes?
But one of the old men mutters,
    And pushes his plate aside:
'Great God!' he cries, 'but it chokes me!
    For this is the day *she* died.'

The guardians gazed in horror,
    The master's face went white;
'Did a pauper refuse their pudding?'
    'Could their ears believe aright?'
Then the ladies clutched their husbands,
    Thinking the man would die,
Struck by a bolt, or something,
    By the outraged One on high.

But the pauper sat for a moment,
    Then rose 'mid a silence grim,
For the others had ceased to chatter,
    And trembled in every limb.
He looked at the guardians' ladies,
    Then, eyeing their lords, he said,
'I eat not the food of villains
    Whose hands are foul and red:

'Whose victims cry for vengeance
    From their dank, unhallowed graves.'
'He's drunk!' said the workhouse master.
    'Or else he's mad, and raves.'
'Not drunk, or mad,' cried the pauper,
    'But only a hunted beast,
Who, torn by the hounds and mangled,
    Declines the vulture's feast.

'I care not a curse for the guardians,
    And I won't be dragged away.
Just let me have the fit out,
    It's only on Christmas Day
That the black past comes to goad me,
    And prey on my burning brain;
I'll tell you the rest in a whisper, –
    I swear I won't shout again.

'Keep your hands off me, curse you!
    Hear me right out to the end.
You come here to see how the paupers
    The season of Christmas spend.
You come here to watch us feeding,
    As they watch the captured beast.
Hear why a penniless pauper
    Spits on your paltry feast.

'Do you think I will take your bounty,
    And let you smile and think
You're doing a noble action
    With the parish's meat and drink?
Where is my wife, you traitors –
    The poor old wife you slew?
Yes, by the God above us,
    My Nance was killed by you!

'Last winter my wife lay dying,
    Starved in a filthy den;
I had never been to the parish, –
    I came to the parish then.
I swallowed my pride in coming,
    For, ere the ruin came,
I held up my head as a trader,
    And I bore a spotless name.

'I came to the parish, craving
    Bread for a starving wife,
Bread for the woman who'd loved me
    Through fifty years of life;
And what do you think they told me,
    Mocking my awful grief?
That "the House" was open to us,
    But they wouldn't give "out relief".

'I slunk to the filthy alley –
    'Twas a cold, raw Christmas eve –
And the bakers' shops were open,
    Tempting a man to thieve;
But I clenched my fists together,
    Holding my head awry;
So I came to her empty-handed,
    And mournfully told her why.

'Then I told her "the House" was open;
   She had heard of the ways of *that*,
For her bloodless cheeks went crimson,
   And up in her rags she sat,
Crying, "Bide the Christmas here, John,
   We've never had one apart;
I think I can bear the hunger, –
   The other would break my heart."

'All through that eve I watched her,
   Holding her hand in mine,
Praying the Lord, and weeping
   Till my lips were salt as brine.
I asked her once if she hungered,
   And as she answered "No,"
The moon shone in at the window
   Set in a wreath of snow.

'Then the room was bathed in glory,
   And I saw in my darling's eyes
The far-away look of wonder
   That comes when the spirit flies;
And her lips were parched and parted,
   And her reason came and went,
For she raved of our home in Devon,
   Where our happiest days were spent.

'And the accents, long forgotten,
   Came back to the tongue once more,
For she talked like the country lassie
   I woo'd by the Devon shore.
Then she rose to her feet and trembled,
   And fell on the rug and moaned,
And "Give me a crust – I'm famished –
   For the love of God!" she groaned.

'I rushed from the room like a madman,
    And flew to the workhouse gate,
Crying, "Food for a dying woman!"
    And the answer came, "Too late."
They drove me away with curses;
    Then I fought with a dog in the street,
And tore from the mongrel's clutches
    A crust he was trying to eat.

'Back, through the filthy by-lanes!
    Back, through the trampled slush!
Up to the crazy garret,
    Wrapped in an awful hush.
My heart sank down at the threshold,
    And I paused with a sudden thrill,
For there in the silv'ry moonlight
    My Nance lay, cold and still.

'Up to the blackened ceiling
    The sunken eyes were cast –
I knew on those lips all bloodless
    My name had been the last;
She called for her absent husband –
    O God! had I but known –
Had called in vain, and in anguish
    Had died in that den – *alone*.

'Yes, there, in a land of plenty,
    Lay a loving woman dead,
Cruelly starved and murdered
    For a loaf of the parish bread.
At yonder gate, last Christmas,
    I craved for a human life.
You, who would feast us paupers,
    What of my murdered wife!

'There, get ye gone to your dinners;
    Don't mind me in the least;
Think of the happy paupers
    Eating your Christmas feast;
And when you recount their blessings
    In your smug parochial way,
Say what you did for *me*, too,
    Only last Christmas Day!'

The Lament of the Ostrich

The Ostrich raised her head and said: 'There's one good reason
I feel so very gloomy at the Christmas Season.
The cards are full of festive fun and oh! so jolly
With robins, snowmen, Christmas trees and boughs of holly –
But one thing's always missing, and I find it hard:
You never see an ostrich on a Christmas card!'

The Ostrich at the window saw the best of sights:
A decorated Christmas tree with gleaming lights.
She said: 'There's lots of baubles and a fairy queen
And ribbons, stars and tinsel on the leaves so green
But one thing's always missing, for it seems to me
You never see an ostrich on a Christmas tree!'

The Ostrich in the schoolyard through the window stared;
A play of the Nativity was being prepared.
She said: 'Oh, how those children love this annual do,
All dressed in beards and angels' wings and robes of blue.
There's an ass, an ox and camels, but I have to say
You never see an ostrich in a Christmas play!'

The Ostrich went to Santa at the far North Pole
And heard him moan: 'I cannot play my usual role –
One reindeer caught a bug and now they've all got flu.
The stockings will be empty, but what *can* I do?'
The Ostrich put the reins on and cried: 'Let's away!
For now at last an ostrich draws the Christmas sleigh!'

The Burning Babe

As I in hoary winter's night stood shivering in the snow,
Surprised I was with sudden heat which made my heart to glow;
And lifting up a fearful eye to view what fire was near,
A pretty Babe all burning bright did in the air appear,
Who, scorched with excessive heat, such floods of tears did
   shed,
As though his floods should quench His flames which with
   His tears were fed.
'Alas,' quoth he, 'but newly born in fiery heats I fry,
Yet none approach to warm their hearts or feel my fire but I.
My faultless breast the furnace is, the fuel wounding thorns;
Love is the fire, and sighs the smoke, the ashes shame and
   scorns;
The fuel Justice layeth on, and Mercy blows the coals;
The metal in this furnace wrought are men's defiled souls
For which, as now on fire I am to work them to their good,
So will I melt into a bath to wash them in my blood.'
With this He vanished out of sight, and swiftly shrunk away,
And straight I called unto mind that it was Christmas day.

New Heaven, New War

Come to your heaven, you heavenly choirs!
Earth hath the heaven of your desires:
Remove your dwelling to your God;
A stall is now His best abode.
Sith men their homage do deny,
Come, angels, all their fault supply.

His chilling cold doth heat require:
Come, seraphins, in lieu of fire;
This little ark no cover hath:
Let cherubs' wings His body swathe.
Come, Raphael, this Babe must eat:
Provide our little Toby meat.

Let Gabriel be now His groom,
That first took up His earthly room;
Let Michael stand in his defence
Whom love hath linked to feeble sense;
Let graces rock when He doth cry,
And angels sing His lullaby.

The same you saw in heavenly seat
Is He that now sucks Mary's teat:
Agnize your king a mortal wight –
His borrowed weed lets not your sight.
Come, kiss the manger where He lies,
That is your bliss above the skies.

This little Babe, so few days old,
Is come to rifle Satan's fold:
All hell doth at His presence quake,
Though He Himself for cold do shake;
For in this weak, unarmed wise
The gates of hell He will surprise.

With tears He fights and wins the field,
His naked breast stands for a shield;
His battering shot are babish cries,
His arrows looks of weeping eyes;
His martial ensigns cold and need,
And feeble flesh His warrior's steed.

His camp is pitched in a stall,
His bulwark but a broken wall;
The crib His trench, hay-stalks His stakes;
Of shepherds He His muster makes;
And thus, as sure His foes to wound,
The angels' trumps alarum sound.

My soul, with Christ join thou in fight;
Stick to the tents that He hath pight;
Within His crib is surest ward:
This little Babe will be thy guard.
If thou wilt foil thy foes with joy,
Then flit not from this heavenly boy.

Christmas at Sea

The sheets were frozen hard, and they cut the naked hand;
The decks were like a slide, where a seaman scarce could stand,
The wind was a nor'-wester, blowing squally off the sea;
And cliffs and spouting breakers were the only things a-lee.

They heard the surf a-roaring before the break of day;
But 'twas only with the peep of light we saw how ill we lay.
We tumbled every hand on deck instanter, with a shout,
And we gave her the maintops'l, and stood by to go about.

All day we tack'd and tack'd between the South Head and the
    North;
All day we hauled the frozen sheets, and got no further forth;
All day as cold as charity, in bitter pain and dread,
For very life and nature we tack'd from head to head.

We gave the South a wider berth, for there the tide-race roared;
But every tack we made we brought the North Head close
    aboard;
So's we saw the cliffs and houses, and the breakers running
    high,
And the coastguard in his garden, with his glass against his eye.

The frost was on the village roofs as white as ocean foam;
The good red fires were burning bright in every 'longshore
    home;
The windows sparkled clear, and the chimneys volley'd out;
And I vow we sniff'd the victuals as the vessel went about.

The bells upon the church were rung with a mighty jovial
    cheer;
For it's just that I should tell you how (of all days in the year)
This day of our adversity was blessed Christmas morn,
And the house above the coastguard's was the house where I
    was born.

O well I saw the pleasant room, the pleasant faces there,
My mother's silver spectacles, my father's silver hair;
And well I saw the firelight, like a flight of homely elves,
Go dancing round the china-plates that stand upon the shelves!

And well I knew the talk they had, the talk that was of me,
Of the shadow on the household and the son that went to sea;
And O the wicked fool I seem'd, in every kind of way,
To be here and hauling frozen ropes on blessed Christmas Day.

They lit the high sea-light, and the dark began to fall.
'All hands to loose topgallant sails!' I heard the captain call.
'By the Lord, she'll never stand it,' our first mate Jackson cried.
... 'It's the one way or the other, Mr Jackson,' he replied.

She stagger'd to her bearings, but the sails were new and good,
And the ship smelt up to windward just as though she
    understood.
As the winter's day was ending, in the entry of the night,
We clear'd the weary headland, and pass'd below the light.

And they heav'd a mighty breath, every soul on board but me,
As they saw her nose again pointing handsome out to sea;
But all that I could think of, in the darkness and the cold,
Was just that I was leaving home, and my folks were growing
    old.

Three Damsels in the Queen's Chamber
Suggested by a drawing of Mr D. G. Rossetti's

Three damsels in the queen's chamber,
   The queen's mouth was most fair;
She spake a word of God's mother
   As the combs went in her hair.
      Mary that is of might,
      Bring us to thy Son's sight.

They held the gold combs out from her
   A span's length off her head;
She sang this song of God's mother
   And of her bearing-bed.
      Mary most full of grace,
      Bring us to thy Son's face.

When she sat at Joseph's hand,
   She looked against her side;
And either way from the short silk band
   Her girdle was all wried.
      Mary that all-good may,
      Bring us to thy Son's way.

Mary had three women for her bed,
   The twain were maidens clean;
The first of them had white and red,
   The third had riven green.
      Mary that is so sweet,
      Bring us to thy Son's feet.

She had three women for her hair,
   Two were gloved soft and shod;
The third had feet and fingers bare,
   She was the likest God.
      Mary that wieldeth land,
      Bring us to thy Son's hand.

She had three women for her ease,
    The twain were good women;
The first two were the two Maries,
    The third was Magdalen.
        Mary that perfect is,
        Bring us to thy Son's kiss.

Joseph had three workmen in his stall,
    To serve him well upon;
The first of them were Peter and Paul,
    The third of them was John.
        Mary, God's handmaiden,
        Bring us to thy Son's ken.

'If your child be none other man's,
    But if it be very mine,
The bedstead shall be gold two spans,
    The bed-foot silver fine'.
        Mary that made God's mirth,
        Bring us to thy Son's birth.

'If the child be some other man's,
    And if it be none of mine,
The manger shall be straw two spans,
    Betwixen kine and kine'.
        Mary that made sin cease,
        Bring us to thy Son's peace.

Christ was born upon this wise,
    It fell on such a night,
Neither with sounds of psalteries,
    Nor with fire for light.
        Mary that is God's spouse,
        Bring us to thy Son's house.

The star came out upon the east
   With a great sound and sweet:
Kings gave gold to make Him feast
   And myrrh for Him to eat.
      Mary of thy sweet mood,
      Bring us to thy Son's good.

He had two handmaids at His head,
   One handmaid at His feet;
The twain of them were fair and red,
   The third one was right sweet.
      Mary that is most wise,
      Bring us to thy Son's eyes.   Amen.

A Christmas Lullaby

Sleep, Baby, sleep! The Mother sings;
Heaven's angels kneel and fold their wings.
    Sleep, Baby, sleep!

With swathes of scented hay Thy bed
By Mary's hand at eve was spread.
    Sleep, Baby, sleep!

At midnight came the shepherds, they
Whom seraphs wakened by the way.
  Sleep, Baby, sleep!

And three kings from the East afar
Ere dawn came guided by Thy star.
  Sleep, Baby, sleep!

They brought Thee gifts of gold and gems,
Pure orient pearls, rich diadems.
  Sleep, Baby, sleep!

But Thou who liest slumbering there
Art King of kings, earth, ocean, air.
  Sleep, Baby, sleep!

Sleep, Baby, sleep! The shepherds sing:
Through heaven, through earth, hosannas ring.
  Sleep, Baby, sleep!

Carol, for Candlemas Day

(published 1661)

Christmas hath made an end,
   Welladay, welladay;
Which was my dearest friend,
   More is the pity.
For with an heavy heart
Must I from thee depart
To follow plough and cart
   All the year after.

Lent is coming fast on,
   Welladay, welladay,
That loves not anyone,
   More is the pity.
For I doubt both my cheeks
Will look thin eating leeks:
Wise is he then that seeks
   For a friend in a corner.

All our good cheer is gone,
   Welladay, welladay;
And turnèd to a bone,
   More is the pity.
In my good master's house
I shall eat no more souse:
Then give me one carouse,
   Gentle kind butler.

It grieves me to the heart,
   Welladay, welladay,
From my friend to depart,
   More is the pity:
Christmas, I mean, 'tis thee,
That thus forsaketh me;
Yet till one hour I see
   Will I be merry.

from *In Memoriam A.H.H.*

Poem 28

The time draws near the birth of Christ:
   The moon is hid; the night is still;
   The Christmas bells from hill to hill
Answer each other in the mist.

Four voices of four hamlets round,
   From far and near, on mead and moor,
   Swell out and fail, as if a door
Were shut between me and the sound:

Each voice four changes on the wind,
   That now dilate, and now decrease,
   Peace and goodwill, goodwill and peace,
Peace and goodwill, to all mankind.

This year I slept and woke with pain,
   I almost wished no more to wake,
   And that my hold on life would break
Before I heard those bells again:

But they my troubled spirit rule,
   For they controlled me when a boy;
   They bring me sorrow touched with joy,
The merry bells of Yule.

from *In Memoriam A.H.H.*

Poem 29

With such compelling cause to grieve
  As daily vexes household peace,
  And chains regret to his decease,
How dare we keep our Christmas-eve;

Which brings no more a welcome guest
  To enrich the threshold of the night
  With showered largess of delight
In dance and song and game and jest?

Yet go, and while the holly boughs
  Entwine the cold baptismal font,
  Make one wreath more for Use and Wont,
That guard the portals of the house;

Old sisters of a day gone by,
  Grey nurses, loving nothing new;
  Why should they miss their yearly due
Before their time? They too will die.

from *In Memoriam A.H.H.*

Poem 30

With trembling fingers did we weave
    The holly round the Christmas hearth;
    A rainy cloud possessed the earth,
And sadly fell our Christmas-eve.

At our old pastimes in the hall
  We gambolled, making vain pretence
  Of gladness, with an awful sense
Of one mute Shadow watching all.

We paused: the winds were in the beech:
  We heard them sweep the winter land;
  And in a circle, hand-in-hand
Sat silent, looking each at each.

Then echo-like our voices rang;
  We sung, though every eye was dim,
  A merry song we sang with him
Last year: impetuously we sang:

We ceased: a gentler feeling crept
  Upon us: surely rest is meet:
  'They rest,' we said, 'their sleep is sweet,'
And silence followed, and we wept.

Our voices took a higher range;
  Once more we sang: 'They do not die
  Nor lose their mortal sympathy,
Nor change to us, although they change;

'Rapt from the fickle and the frail
  With gathered power, yet the same,
  Pierces the keen seraphic flame
From orb to orb, from veil to veil.'

Rise, happy morn, rise, holy morn,
  Draw forth the cheerful day from night:
  O Father, touch the east, and light
The light that shone when Hope was born.

On Christmas Day

Shall dumpish melancholy spoil my joys
     While angels sing
     And mortals ring
   My Lord and Saviour's praise?
Awake from sloth, for that alone destroys:
'Tis sin defiles, 'tis sloth puts out thy joys.
  See how they run from place to place,
  And seek for ornaments of grace;
  Their houses decked with sprightly green
  In winter makes a summer seen;
    They bays and holly bring
     As if 'twere spring!

Shake off thy sloth, my drowsy soul: awake!
     With angels sing
     Unto thy King,
   And pleasant music make.

Thy lute, thy harp, or else thy heart-strings, take,
And with thy music let thy senses wake.
  See how each one the other calls
  To fix his ivy on the walls.
  Transplanted there, it seems to grow
  As if it rooted were below:
    Thus He, who is thy King,
      Makes winter, spring.

Shall houses clad in summer liveries
        His praises sing
        And laud thy King,
      And wilt not thou arise?
Forsake thy bed, and grow (my soul) more wise.
Attire thyself in cheerful liveries:
  Let pleasant branches still be seen
  Adorning thee, both quick and green;
  And – which with glory better suits –
  Be laden all the year with fruits,
    Inserted into Him,
      For ever spring.

'Tis He that life and spirit doth infuse:
        Let everything
        The praises sing
        Of Christ, the King of Jews,
Who makes things green, and with a spring infuse
A season which to see it doth not use:
  Old Winter's frost and hoary hair
  With garlands crowned, bays doth wear;
  The nipping frost of wrath being gone,
  To Him the manger made a throne,
    Due praises let us sing,
      Winter and spring.

See how, their bodies clad with finer clothes,
        They now begin
        His praises to sing
        Who purchased their repose,

Whereby their inward joy they do disclose.
Their dress alludes to better works than those:
   His gayer weeds and finer band,
   New suit and hat, into his hand
   The ploughman takes; his neatest shoes
   And warmer gloves he means to use:
     And shall not I, my King,
       Thy praises sing?

See how their breath doth smoke, and how they haste
      His praise to sing
      With cherubim;
   They scarce a breakfast taste,
But through the streets, lest precious time should waste,
When service doth begin, to church they haste.
   And shall not I, Lord, come to Thee,
   The beauty of Thy temple see?
   Thy name with joy I will confess,
   Clad in my Saviour's righteousness;
     'Mong all Thy servants sing
       To Thee, my King.

'Twas Thou that gave us cause for fine attires;
      Even Thou, O King,
      As in the spring,
   Dost warm us with Thy fires
Of love: Thy blood hath bought us new desires;
Thy righteousness doth clothe with new attires.
   Both fresh and fine let me appear
   This day divine, to close the year;
   Among the rest let me be seen
   A living branch and always green;
     Think it a pleasant thing
       Thy praise to sing.

At break of day, O how the bells did ring!
      To Thee, my King,
      The bells did ring!
     To Thee the angels sing:

Thy goodness did produce this other spring,
For this it is they make the bells to ring:
   The sounding bells do through the air
   Proclaim Thy welcome far and near,
   While I alone with Thee inherit
   All these joys beyond my merit.
     Who would not always sing
      To such a King?

I all these joys, above my merit, see
     By Thee, my King,
     To whom I sing,
    Entire conveyed to me.
My treasure, Lord, Thou makest the people be
That I with pleasure might Thy servants see.
   Even in their rude external ways
   They do set forth my Saviour's praise,
   And minister a light to me;
   While I by them do hear to Thee
     Praises, my Lord and King,
      Whole churches ring.

Hark how remoter parishes do sound!
     Far off they ring
     For Thee, my King,
    Even round about the town:
The churches scattered over all the ground
Serve for Thy praise, who art with glory crowned.
   This city is an engine great
   That makes my pleasure more complete;
   The sword, the mace, the magistrate,
   To honour Thee attend in state;
     The whole assembly sings;
      The minster rings.

'Now Thrice Welcome, Christmas'
(published 1695)

Now thrice welcome, Christmas,
  Which brings us good cheer,
Minced pies and plum porridge,
  Good ale and strong beer;
With pig, goose and capon,
  The best that may be,
So well doth the weather
  And our stomachs agree.

Observe how the chimneys
  Do smoke all about:
The cooks are providing
  For dinner, no doubt;
But those on whose tables
  No victuals appear –
Oh may they keep Lent
  All the rest of the year!

With holly and ivy
  So green and so gay,
We deck up our houses
  As fresh as the day,
With bay and rosemary
  And laurels complete,
And every one now
  Is a king in conceit.

Christ's Nativity

Awake, glad heart, get up and sing:
It is the birthday of thy King!
      Awake, awake!
      The sun doth shake
Light from his locks, and all the way
Breathing perfumes, doth spice the day.

Awake, awake! Hark how the wood rings,
Winds whisper, and the busy springs
      A consort make.
      Awake, awake!
Man is their high priest, and should rise
To offer up the sacrifice.

I would I were some bird, or star,
Fluttering in woods, or lifted far
      Above this inn
      And road of sin!
Then either star or bird should be
Shining, or singing, still to Thee.

I would I had in my best part
Fit rooms for Thee, or that my heart
      Were so clean as
      Thy manger was.
But I am all filth, and obscene:
Yet, if thou wilt, thou canst make clean.

Sweet Jesu, will then: let no more
This leper haunt and soil Thy door:
      Cure him, ease him,
      O release him!
And let once more by mystic birth
The Lord of life be born in earth.

The Nativity

Written in the Year 1656

Peace? And to all the world? Sure, one –
And He the Prince of Peace – hath none.
He travels to be born, and then
Is born to travel more again.
Poor Galilee! Thou canst not be
The place for His nativity:
His restless mother's called away,
And not delivered till she pay.
   A tax? 'Tis so still! We can see
The Church thrive in her misery
And, like her head at Bethlem, rise
When she oppressed with troubles lies.
Rise? Should all fall, we cannot be
In more extremities than He.
Great type of passions, come what will,
Thy grief exceeds all copies still.
Thou cam'st from heaven to earth that we
Might go from earth to heaven with Thee;
And though Thou found'st no welcome here,
Thou didst provide us mansions there.
A stable was Thy court, and when
Men turned to beasts, beasts would be men.
They were Thy courtiers, others none;
And their poor manger was Thy throne.
No swaddling silks Thy limbs did fold,
Though Thou couldst turn Thy rays to gold.
No rockers waited on Thy birth,
No cradles stirred, nor songs of mirth;
But her chaste lap and sacred breast
Which lodged Thee first did give Thee rest.

But stay: what light is that doth stream
And drop here in a gilded beam?
It is Thy star runs page, and brings
Thy tributary eastern kings.
Lord, grant some light to us, that we
May with them find the way to Thee.
Behold what mists eclipse the day:
How dark it is! Shed down one ray
To guide us out of this sad night,
And say once more, *Let there be light*.

'Now that the Time is Come'

(published 1700)

Now that the time is come wherein
  Our Saviour, Christ, was born,
The larder's full of beef and pork,
  The garner's filled with corn;
As God hath plenty to thee sent,
  Take comfort in thy labours,
And let it never thee repent
  To feast thy needy neighbours.

Let fires in every chimney be
  That people they may warm them;
Tables with dishes covered –
  Good victuals will not harm them.
With mutton, veal, beef, pig and pork,
  Well furnish every board;
Plum-pudding, furmity and what
  Thy stock will them afford.

No niggard of thy liquor be,
  Let it go round thy table;
People may freely drink, but not
  So long as they are able.
Good customs they may be abused,
  Which makes rich men to slack us;
This feast is to relieve the poor
  And not to drunken Bacchus.

Thus if thou doest
  'Twill credit raise thee;
God will thee bless
  And neighbours praise thee.

'Christmas Day is Come...'

Christmas Day is come; let's all prepare for mirth,
  Which fills the heavens and earth at this amazing birth.
Through both, the joyous angels in strife and hurry fly
  With glory and hosannas – 'All holy' they do cry.
In heaven the Church Triumphant adores with all her choirs,
  The Militant on earth with humble faith admires.

But why should we rejoice? Should we not rather mourn
  To see the hope of nations thus in a stable born?
Where are His crown and sceptre, where His throne sublime,
  Where is His train majestic, that should the stars outshine?
Is there not sumptuous palace, nor any inn at all,
  To lodge His heavenly mother but in a filthy stall?

'Come, Thou Long-Expected Jesus'

Come, Thou long-expected Jesus,
　　Born to set Thy people free;
From our fears and sins relieve us,
　　Let us find our rest in Thee:
Israel's strength and consolation,
　　Hope of all the earth Thou art;
Dear desire of every nation,
　　Joy of every living heart.

Born Thy people to deliver,
　　Born a Child and yet a King;
Born to reign in us for ever,
　　Now Thy gracious kingdom bring;
By Thine own eternal Spirit
　　Rule in all our hearts alone,
By Thine all-sufficient merit
　　Raise us to Thy glorious throne.

A Christmas Carol

So, now is come our joyfullest feast –
Let every man be jolly:
Each room with ivy leaves is dressed,
And every post with holly.
　　Though some churls at our mirth repine,
　　Round your foreheads garlands twine;
　　Drown sorrow in a cup of wine,
And let us all be merry.

Now all our neighbours' chimneys smoke,
And Christmas blocks are burning;
Their ovens they with baked meats choke,
And all their spits are turning.
　　Without the door let sorrow lie,
　　And if, for cold, it hap to die,
　　We'll bury it in a Christmas pie,
And ever more be merry.

Now every lad is wondrous trim,
And no man minds his labour;
Our lasses have provided them
A bagpipe and a tabor.
  Young men, and maids, and girls and boys,
  Give life to one anothers' joys,
  And you anon shall by their noise
Perceive that they are merry.

Rank misers now do sparing shun,
Their hall of music soundeth;
And dogs thence with whole shoulders run,
So all things there aboundeth.
  The country folk themselves advance,
  For crowdy-mutton's come out of France;
  And Jack shall pipe and Jill shall dance,
And all the town be merry.

Ned Swash hath fetched his bands from pawn,
And all his best apparel;
Brisk Nell hath brought a ruff of lawn
With droppings of the barrel;
   And those that hardly all the year
   Had bread to eat or rags to wear
   Will have both clothes and dainty fare,
And all the day be merry.

Now poor men to the justices
With capons make their arrants,
And if they hap to fail of these,
They plague them with their warrants.
   But now they feed them with good cheer,
   And what they want they take in beer,
   For *Christmas comes but once a year*:
And then they shall be merry.

Good farmers, in the country, nurse
The poor that else were undone;
Some landlords spend their money worse
On lust and pride in London.
   There the roisterers they do play,
   Drab and dice their lands away,
   Which may be ours another day:
And therefore let's be merry.

The client now his suit forbears,
The prisoner's heart is eased;
The debtor drinks away his cares
And, for the time, is pleased.
   Though other purses be more fat,
   Why should we pine or grieve at that?
   Hang sorrow, care will kill a cat:
And therefore let's be merry.

Hark how the wags abroad do call
Each other forth to rambling:

Anon you'll see them in the hall
For nuts and apples scrambling.
　　Hark how the roofs with laughters sound:
　　Anon they'll think the house goes round
　　For they the cellar's depth have found –
And there they will be merry.

The wenches with their wassail bowls
About the streets are singing:
The boys are come to catch the owls,
The wild mare in is bringing.
　　Our kitchen boy hath broke his box
　　And, to the dealing of the ox,
　　Our honest neighbours come by flocks,
And there they will be merry.

Now kings and queens poor sheep cotes have
And mate with everybody:
The honest now may play the knave,
And wise men play at Noddy.
　　Some youths will now a-mumming go,
　　Some others play at rowland-hoe
　　And twenty other gameboys more
Because they will be merry.

Then wherefore, in these merry days
Should we, I pray, be duller?
No; let us sing some roundelays
To make our mirth the fuller.
　　And, whilest thus inspired we sing,
　　Let all the street with echoes ring:
　　Woods, and hills, and everything
Bear witness we are merry.

from *The River Duddon: A Series of Sonnets*

To the Rev. Dr Wordsworth

The minstrels played their Christmas tune
Tonight beneath my cottage eaves,
While, smitten by a lofty moon,
The encircling laurels, thick with leaves,
Gave back a rich and dazzling sheen
That overpowered their natural green.

Through hill and valley every breeze
Had sunk to rest with folded wings:
Keen was the air, but could not freeze,
Nor check, the music of the strings;
So stout and hardy were the band
That scraped the chords with strenuous hand!

And who but listened? – till was paid
Respect to every inmate's claim:
The greeting given, the music played,
In honour of each household name,
Duly pronounced with lusty call,
And 'Merry Christmas' wished to all!

O brother, I revere the choice
That took thee from thy native hills;
And it is given thee to rejoice,
Though public care full often tills
(Heaven only witness of the toil)
A barren and ungrateful soil.

Yet, would that thou, with me and mine,
Hadst heard this never-failing rite,
And seen on other faces shine
A true revival of the light
Which Nature and these rustic powers
In simple childhood spread through ours!

For pleasure hath not ceased to wait
On these expected annual rounds;
Whether the rich man's sumptuous gate
Call forth the unelaborate sounds,
Or they are offered at the door
That guards the lowliest of the poor.

How touching when, at midnight, sweep
Snow-muffled winds, and all is dark,
To hear – and sink again to sleep!
Or, at an earlier call, to mark,
By blazing fire, the still suspense
Of self-complacent innocence;

The mutual nod – the grave disguise
Of hearts with gladness brimming o'er;
And some unbidden tears that rise
For names once heard, and heard no more:
Tears brightened by the serenade
For infant in the cradle laid.

Ah! not for emerald fields alone,
With ambient streams more pure and bright
Than fabled Cytherea's zone
Glittering before the Thunderer's sight,
Is to my heart of hearts endeared
The ground where we were born and reared!

Hail, ancient manners! sure defence,
Where they survive, of wholesome laws;
Remnants of love whose modest sense
Thus into narrow room withdraws;
Hail, usages of pristine mould,
And ye that guard them, mountains old ...

'O You Merry, Merry Souls'
(published 1740)

O you merry, merry souls,
    Christmas is a-coming;
We shall have flowing bowls,
    Dancing, piping, drumming.

Delicate minced pies
    To feast every virgin,
Capon and goose likewise,
    Brawn and a dish of sturgeon.

Then, for your Christmas box,
    Sweet plum cakes and money,
Delicate holland smocks,
    Kisses sweet as honey.

Hey for the Christmas ball,
    Where we shall be jolly;
Jigging short and tall,
    Kate, Dick, Ralph and Molly.

Then to the hop we'll go,
    Where we'll jig and caper;
Maidens all-a-row;
    Will shall play the scraper.

Hodge shall dance with Prue,
    Keeping time with kisses;
We'll have a jovial crew
    Of sweet smirking misses.

The Cherry Tree Carol
(published 1823)

I

Joseph was an old man,
 And an old man was he,
When he wedded Mary
 In the land of Galilee.

When Joseph was married,
 And Mary home had got,
Mary proved with child,
 By whom Joseph knew not.

Joseph and Mary walked
 Through an orchard good,
Where was cherries and berries,
 So red as any blood.

Joseph and Mary walked
 Through an orchard green,
Where was berries and cherries,
 As thick as might be seen.

O then bespoke Mary,
 So meek and so mild:
'Pluck me one cherry, Joseph,
 For I am with child.'

O then bespoke Joseph,
 With words most unkind:
'Let him pluck thee a cherry
 That brought thee with child.'

O then bespoke the Babe
   Within His mother's womb:
'Bow down then the tallest tree
   For my mother to have some.'

Then bowed down the highest tree
   Unto His mother's hand;
Then she cried: 'See, Joseph,
   I have cherries at command.'

O then bespoke Joseph:
   'I have done Mary wrong;
But cheer up, my dearest,
   And be not cast down.

'O eat your cherries, Mary,
   O eat your cherries now;
O eat your cherries, Mary,
   That grow upon the bough.'

Then Mary plucked a cherry
   As red as the blood;
Then Mary went home
   With her heavy load.

II

As Joseph was a-walking,
   He heard an angel sing:
'This night shall be born
   our heavenly King;

'He neither shall be borned
   In housen nor in hall,
Nor in the place of paradise,
   But in an ox's stall.

'He neither shall be clothed
   In purple nor in pall,
But all in fair linen,
   As were babies all.

'He neither shall be rocked
   In silver nor in gold,
But in a wooden cradle,
   That rocks on the mould.

'He neither shall be christened
   In white wine nor red,
But with fair spring water,
   With which we were christened.'

III

Then Mary took her young Son
   And set Him on her knee:
'I pray Thee now, dear Child,
   Tell how this world shall be.'

'O, I shall be as dead, mother,
   As the stones in the wall;
O the stones in the streets, mother,
   Shall mourn for me all.

'And upon a Wednesday
   My vow I will make,
And upon Good Friday
   My death I will take.

'Upon Easter day, mother,
   My uprising shall be;
O the sun and the moon, mother,
   Shall both rise with me.'

'The Moon Shines Bright'

(nineteenth century)

The moon shines bright, and the stars give a light:
    A little before it was day,
Our Lord, our God, He called on us,
    And bid us wake and pray.

Awake, awake, good people all,
    Awake, and you shall hear,
Our Lord, our God, He died on the cross
    For us whom He loved so dear.

O fair, O fair Jerusalem,
    When shall I come to thee?
When shall my sorrows have an end,
    Thy joy that I may see?

The fields were green as green could be,
    When from His glorious seat
Our Lord, our God, He watered us
    With His heavenly dew so sweet.

And for the saving of our souls
    Christ died upon the cross;
We ne'er shall do for Jesus Christ
    As He has done for us.

The life of man is but a span,
  And cut down in its flower;
We are here today and tomorrow are gone,
  We are all dead in an hour.

O pray, teach your children, man,
  The while that you are here;
It will be better for your souls
  When your corpse lies on the bier.

Today you may be alive, dear man,
  Worth many a thousand pound;
Tomorrow may be dead, dear man,
  And your body be laid under ground.

With one turf at your head, O man,
  And another at your feet,
Thy good deeds and thy bad, O man,
  Will all together meet.

My song is done, I must be gone,
  I can no longer here.
God bless you all, both great and small,
  And send you a happy new year!

'Softly the Night is Sleeping...'

(twentieth century, Sussex traditional)

Softly the night is sleeping on Bethlehem's peaceful hill,
Silent the shepherds watching their gentle flocks are still.
But hark the wondrous music falls from the opening sky,
Valley and cliff re-echo glory to God on high.
Glory to God it rings again,
Peace on the earth, goodwill to men.

Come with the gladsome shepherds quick hastening from the
   fold,
Come with the wise men bringing incense and myrrh and gold,
Come to Him poor and lowly, all round the cradle throng,
Come with our hearts of sunshine and sing the angels' song.
Glory to God tell out again,
Peace on the earth, goodwill to men.

Wave ye the wreath unfading, the fir tree and the pine,
Green from the snows of winter to deck the holy shrine;
Bring ye the happy children for this is Christmas morn,
Jesus the sinless infant, Jesus the Lord is born.
Glory to God, to God again,
Peace on the earth, goodwill to men.

⁓ *List of Latin translations*

Note: titles are in alphabetical order, and not necessarily the order in which they appear in this volume.

'**Adam Lay Ybounden**'. *Deo gracias:* 'thanks be to God'.

'**Be Merry, all that be Present**'. *Omnes de Saba venient:* 'all they from Sheba shall come' is from Isaiah 60:6 (part of the first reading for the Mass for Epiphany; also employed as the gradual for the same service in the Sarum – or Salisbury – rite used throughout the south of England).

Eia, Jesus hodie natus est de Virgine. The title means 'Rejoice! today Jesus is born of the Virgin'. In the same poem we have *non ex virile semine:* 'not from the seed of man'; *pro peccante homine:* 'for sinful man'; *stella ducte lumine:* 'by a star's guiding light'; *gloria tibi, Domine:* 'glory to you, O Lord'; *ullo sine crimine:* 'without any offence (or fault)'.

'*Nova, Nova: "Ave" Fit ex "Eva"*'. The title means 'news, news: [the word] "Hail" derives from "Eve"'. Employing a commonplace, this explains that the initial word of greeting used by the angel Gabriel to Mary when he tells her that she is pregnant ('Hail, thou that art highly favoured': Luke 1:28) contains the same letters in Latin as the Latin form of the name Eve: Mary is thus the second Eve, come to repair the damage wrought by the first in the Garden of Eden when she plucked the fruit from the tree of knowledge (Genesis 3). The Latin in the concluding stanza, *ecce ancilla Domini* ('behold the handmaid of the Lord'), is from Mary's reply to Gabriel at Luke 1:38.

Regina Coeli (by Coventry Patmore). The title means: ' Queen of heaven'.

'*Rorate Coeli Desuper*' (by William Dunbar). The title means 'drop down dew from above, you heavens' and comes from Isaiah 45:8, used as a response in the services for the fourth Sunday in Advent (dew is an emblem of divine grace). The refrain, *et nobis puer natus est*, means 'and a boy is born for us'

(Isaiah 9:6; also used in the Christmas services). The variant in stanzas 3 and 7, *pro nobis puer natus est* means 'for us a boy is born,' and that in stanzas 4 and 6, *qui nobis puer natus est*, 'the boy who is born for us'.

'Saint Stephen was a Clerk'. *Christus natus est:* 'Christ is born'.

'The Boar's Head'. *Caput apri defero, reddens laudes Domino:* 'I bear the boar's head, giving praises to the Lord'; *qui estis in convivio:* 'who are present at this feast'; *servite cum cantico:* 'deliver and guard it with a song'.

'There is no Rose'. *Res miranda:* 'a thing to be marvelled at'; *pari forma:* 'of the same form'; *gloria in excelsis Deo:* 'glory to God in the highest'; *gaudeamus:* 'let us rejoice'; *transeamus:* 'let us depart'.

'To Bliss God Bring Us'. The poem is particularly rich in liturgical quotations: *Christe redemptor omnium:* 'O Christ, redeemer of all' (from a hymn for Christmas mattins); *iam lucis orto sidere:* 'now by the rising of the morning star' (Christ: Revelation 22:16, also used in a hymn for the first Sunday in Advent); *a solis ortus cardine:* 'from the point of the sun's rising' (from a hymn for Christmas lauds); *O lux beata Trinitas:* 'O blessed threefold light' (from a hymn for the first Sunday after Trinity); *exultet coelum laudibus:* 'let heaven resound with praises' (from a hymn used for apostles' days).

∼ *Index of first lines*

⌣ Acknowledgements

The editor and publisher would like to thank the following for permission to reproduce copyright, and anonymous archive and library, material:

The Master and Fellows of Balliol College, Oxford for 'Be merry all that be present', MS 354; and 'Nova, Nova, "Ave" Fit ex "Eva"', MS 354; Bodleian Library for 'Noel, Noel, Noel' and 'To Bliss God Bring Us, All and Some', MS Eng. poet. e.1; The British Library for 'I Sing of a Maiden', 'Lullay, Mine Liking', 'Out of the Blossom Sprang a Thorn', 'Adam Lay Ybounden', 'Eia, Jesus Hodie', 'St Stephen was a Clerk', BL Sloane MS 2593; 'Nay, Ivy, Nay, It Shall Not Be, Iwis', BL MS Harley 5396; 'Alone, Alone, Alone, Alone' and 'Ah, My Dear, Ah, My Dear Son', BL MS Add. 5465; and Thomas Traherne, 'On Christmas Day' from Poems of Felicity, MS Burney 392; David Higham Associates on behalf of the author for Norman Nicholson, 'Carol' from Five Rivers, Faber and Faber (1944); John Murray Publishers Ltd for John Betjeman, 'Christmas' from Collected Poems by John Betjeman; W. W. Norton & Company for E. E. Cummings, 'little tree' from Complete Poems 1904–1962 by E. E. Cummings, edited by George J. Firmage. Copyright © 1991 by the Trustees for the E. E. Cummings Trust and George James Firmage; Peters, Fraser and Dunlop Group Ltd on behalf of the Estate of the author for Laurie Lee, 'Christmas Landscape' from Selected Poems by Laurie Lee; The Society of Authors on behalf of the Literary Trustees of the author for Walter de la Mare, 'A Ballad of Christmas' from The Complete Poems of Walter de la Mare (1969); Spike Milligan Productions Ltd for Spike Milligan, 'Christmas 1970' from Collected Poems; The Master and Fellows of Trinity College Cambridge for 'There is no Rose', MS 0.3.58; A. P. Watt Ltd on behalf of The Royal Literary Fund for G. K. Chesterton 'A Child of the Snows' from Poems (1915).

Every effort has been made to trace all the copyright holders, but if any have been inadvertently overlooked the publishers will be pleased to make the necessary arrangement at the first opportunity.